First World War
and Army of Occupation
War Diary
France, Belgium and Germany

38 DIVISION
Headquarters, Branches and Services
Commander Royal Engineers
2 December 1915 - 7 June 1919

WO95/2544/1

The Naval & Military Press Ltd
www.nmarchive.com
Published in association with The National Archives

Published by

The Naval & Military Press Ltd

Unit 10 Ridgewood Industrial Park,
Uckfield, East Sussex,
TN22 5QE England
Tel: +44 (0) 1825 749494

www.naval-military-press.com
www.nmarchive.com

This diary has been reprinted in facsimile from the original. Any imperfections are inevitably reproduced and the quality may fall short of modern type and cartographic standards.

© **Crown Copyright**
Images reproduced by permission of The National Archives, London, England, 2015.

Contents

Document type	Place/Title	Date From	Date To
Heading	WO95/2544/1 Commander Royal Engineers		
Heading	38th Division Divl Engineers C.R.E. Dec 1915-Jun 1919		
Heading	C.R.E. 38th Div. Vol I Dec 15		
War Diary	Winchester	02/12/1915	02/12/1915
War Diary	Havre	03/12/1915	04/12/1915
War Diary	St Omer	05/12/1915	05/12/1915
War Diary	Clarques	05/12/1915	19/12/1915
War Diary	St. Venant	20/12/1915	24/01/1916
Heading	War Diary Of Headquarters Royal Engineers 38th Welsh Division From February 1st 1916 To February 29th 1916		
War Diary	Lestrem. R9 A 3.2	01/02/1916	07/02/1916
War Diary	Bethune (Combined Sheet) Edition 6	06/02/1916	14/02/1916
War Diary	Bethune (Combined Sheet) Edition 6	09/02/1916	21/02/1916
War Diary	Locon X.7. Central	17/02/1916	28/02/1916
War Diary	Locon X.7. Central	22/02/1916	28/02/1916
Heading	C.R.E. 38 Div Vol 3 War Diary Of. Headquarters Royal Engineers 38th (Welsh) Division. From March 1st 1916 To March 31st 1916		
War Diary	Locon X 7. Central Bethune Combined Sheet Edition 6	01/03/1916	29/03/1916
Miscellaneous	Report Of Work Done Under C.R.E. 38th Division Week-Ending 1/4/16	01/04/1916	01/04/1916
Miscellaneous	Weekly Report Of Work Under C.R.E. 38th Division.	25/03/1916	25/03/1916
Miscellaneous	11th Corps. Report Of Work Under C.R.E. 38th Division W/E 18/3/16	18/03/1916	18/03/1916
Miscellaneous	Weekly Report of Work done under C.R.E. 38th Division.	11/03/1916	11/03/1916
Miscellaneous	Weekly Report of work done under C.R.E. 38th Division.	04/03/1916	04/03/1916
Diagram etc	Sketch of Bangalore Torpedoe		
Heading	War Diary of Headquarters Royal Engineers 38th Welsh Division for April 1916 C.R.E. 38 D Vol 4		
War Diary	Locon X 7 Central Bethune Combined Map (Edit 6)	12/04/1916	15/04/1916
War Diary	Lagorgue L 35 b 7.9. Sheet 36A France 3 Edition	17/04/1916	17/04/1916
Miscellaneous	Report Of Work Done Under C.R.E. 38th Division w/e 8th April 1916	08/04/1916	08/04/1916
Miscellaneous	Report Of Work Done Under C.R.E. 38th Division Week Ending 15/4/16	15/04/1916	15/04/1916
Miscellaneous	Report Of Work Done Under C.R.E. 38th Division. week-ending 22-4-16	22/04/1916	22/04/1916
Miscellaneous	Weekly Report Of Work Done Under C.R.E. 38th Division w/e 29-4-16	29/04/1916	29/04/1916
Heading	War Diary Headquarters Royal Engineers 38th Welsh Division May 1916 R.E. 38 Div Vol 5		
War Diary	Lagorgue L 35 b7.9 Sheet 36 A France Edition 3	14/05/1916	31/05/1916
Miscellaneous	Weekly Report Of Work Done Under C.R.E. 38th Division.	06/05/1916	06/05/1916
Miscellaneous	Progress Report Of Work Done Under C.R.E. 38th Div.	13/05/1916	13/05/1916

Type	Description	Date From	Date To
Miscellaneous	Progress Report Of Work Done Under C.R.E. 38th Division w/e 20-5-16	20/05/1916	20/05/1916
Miscellaneous	Weekly Progress Of Work Done Under C.R.E. 38th Division w/e 27-5-16	27/05/1916	27/05/1916
Heading	Headquarters Royal Engineers 38th Welsh Division War Diary For June 1916 R.E. 38 Div Vol 6		
War Diary	La Gorgue L 35b 7.9. Sheet 36 A France Edition 3	10/06/1916	13/06/1916
War Diary	T Venant P.H.E.	13/06/1916	15/06/1916
War Diary	St Michel	19/06/1916	19/06/1916
War Diary	T.13 C.O.5 France Sheet 36b	16/06/1916	26/06/1916
War Diary	Ribeaucourt.	27/06/1916	27/06/1916
War Diary	2 1/2 Mls SW of Bernaville Lens Map.	28/06/1916	30/06/1916
Heading	War Diary of Headquarters Royal Engineers 38th Welsh Div July 1916 Vol 7		
War Diary	Rubempre T 13 B 7.1. Sheet 57D (France.)	01/07/1916	01/07/1916
War Diary	Toutencourt U.I Central Sheet 57D (France).	03/07/1916	03/07/1916
War Diary	Mericourt L'Abbe J D Sheet 62D (France)	04/07/1916	05/07/1916
War Diary	Grovetown Camp. Lid Central Sheet Albert Combined France.	06/07/1916	09/07/1916
War Diary	Grovetown Camp.	11/07/1916	11/07/1916
War Diary	Treux J 5 b Albert Combined Sheet	12/07/1916	13/07/1916
War Diary	Pont Remy	13/07/1916	13/07/1916
War Diary	Rubempre	14/07/1916	14/07/1916
War Diary	Couin	15/07/1916	15/07/1916
War Diary	Couin J.I. (Sheet 57D)	23/07/1916	28/07/1916
War Diary	BUS J 26 (Sheet J7d)	29/07/1916	31/07/1916
War Diary	Poperinghe Belgium.	31/07/1916	31/07/1916
War Diary	Esquelbecq C8 Sheet 27	31/07/1916	31/07/1916
Miscellaneous	Report By C.R.E. 38th Division On Operations Between July 5th and 13th 1916	05/07/1916	05/07/1916
Map			
Miscellaneous	Notes On Mametz Wood Obtained By Patrol, 2nd Battn, Royal Irish Regiment, On Night 3/4th. July.	03/07/1916	03/07/1916
Heading	War Diary of Headquarters Royal Engineers 38th Welsh Division August 1916 C.R.E. Vol 8		
War Diary	Esquelbecq C.8. Sheet 27	01/08/1916	02/08/1916
War Diary	Reserve Area VIII Corps	03/08/1916	19/08/1916
War Diary	Esquelbecq C8 Sheet 27	21/08/1916	21/08/1916
War Diary	St Sixte Camp Sheet 28 Aid	21/08/1916	21/08/1916
War Diary	Left Div VIII Corps Area	23/08/1916	23/08/1916
Miscellaneous	Details of Work in Hand 21-31 Aug. 1916	21/08/1916	21/08/1916
Heading	War Diary Headquarters 38th Divisional Engineers September. 1916. R.E. Vol 9		
War Diary	St Sixte Camp Sheet 28 Aid Left Div VIII Corps Area	08/09/1916	16/09/1916
War Diary	St Sixte Camp.	17/09/1916	22/09/1916
Miscellaneous	Summary Of Work. 38th Division Engineers. September. 1916	00/09/1916	00/09/1916
Heading	War Diary-October-1916. Headquarters Royal Engineers 38th (Welsh) Division. Vol 10 31-10-1916		
War Diary	St Sixte Camp Sheet 28 A.I.D. Left Div VIII Corps Area.	03/10/1916	18/10/1916
War Diary	St Sixte Camp.	19/10/1916	30/10/1916
Heading	War Diary November 1916 Headquarters. Royal Engineers 38th Division Vol XI		
War Diary	St Sixte Camp Aid Left Div VIII Corps Area.	16/11/1916	30/11/1916

Miscellaneous	Summary Of Work. 38th Divisional Engineers November. 1916	00/11/1916	00/11/1916
Miscellaneous	Report on Raid Held On Nov 17	18/11/1916	18/11/1916
Diagram etc	Section Of German Parapet.		
Diagram etc	Concrete O.P.		
Heading	War Diary Headquarters Royal Engineers 38th Division December 1916. Vol 12		
War Diary	St Sixte Camp. Sheet 28 Aid Left Des VIII Corps Area.	01/12/1916	14/12/1916
War Diary	Esquelbecq C8 Sheet 27	23/12/1916	30/12/1916
Miscellaneous	Summary Of Work. 38th Division Engineers. October 1916	00/10/1916	00/10/1916
Heading	War Diary Headquarters Royal Engineers 38th Welsh Div January 1917 HQ R.E. 35 D. Vol 13		
War Diary	Esquelbecq Sheet 27 VIII Corps Reserve Div Area	01/01/1917	14/01/1917
War Diary	St Sixte Aid Sheet 28. Left Div VIII Corps Area	15/01/1917	26/01/1917
Heading	War Diary Headquarters Royal Engineers 38th Division February 1917 Vol 14		
War Diary	St Sixte. Aid Sheet 28 Left-Div VIII Corps Area	01/02/1917	28/02/1917
Heading	War Diary Headquarters Royal Engineers 38th Div. March 1917 Vol 15		
War Diary	St Sixte Aid Sheet 28 Left Div VIII Corps Area	02/03/1917	30/03/1917
War Diary	Suzanne	19/12/1917	23/12/1917
War Diary	St Sixte Aid Sheet 28 Left Div VIII Corps Area	06/04/1917	30/04/1917
War Diary	Suzanne	19/12/1917	23/12/1917
War Diary	St. Sixte Aid Sheet 28 Left Div VIII Corps Area	01/05/1917	29/05/1917
Heading	Original War Diary Headquarters Royal Engineers 38th Division 30th June 1917 Vol 18		
War Diary	St. Sixte Camp Aid. Sheet 28 Left Div VIII Corps	10/06/1917	29/06/1917
Heading	Original War Diary Headquarters Royal Engineers 38th Division July 1917 1.8.1917. Vol 19		
War Diary	Norrents Fontes.	01/07/1917	15/07/1917
War Diary	St Hilaire Training Area	16/07/1917	19/07/1917
War Diary	Proven Sheet 27 F.7. Central	20/07/1917	21/07/1917
War Diary	Dragon Camp. Map Ref. Sheet 28	21/07/1917	27/07/1917
War Diary	Dragon Camp. Map Ref. A15.b.5.7. Sheet 28	27/07/1917	30/07/1917
War Diary	Elvedinghe Chateau Sheet 28 B 14 b.2.1	30/07/1917	30/07/1917
War Diary	Forward Battl Div HQs. at Elvedingh Chatu Sheet 28 B 14.b.2.1	31/07/1917	31/07/1917
War Diary	38th Div Hqs (Battl Hqs) Elvedinghe Chatu. Sheet 28 B 14.b.2.1	31/07/1917	31/07/1917
Heading	War Diary August 1917 C.R.E. 38th Division Vol 20		
War Diary	Elvedinghe Chatu Map ref. Sheet 28 B 14, b.2.1	01/08/1917	02/08/1917
War Diary	Dragon Camp. Map Ref Sheet 28 A 15.b.5.7	03/08/1917	20/08/1917
War Diary	Elvedinghe Chatu	20/08/1917	31/08/1917
Heading	Original War Diary September 1917. Headquarters Royal Engineers 38th Division Vol 21 1.10.17		
War Diary	Elverdinghe Chateau	01/09/1917	11/09/1917
War Diary	Proven.	12/09/1917	16/09/1917
War Diary	Croix Du Bac	17/09/1917	30/09/1917
Operation(al) Order(s)	C.R.E. 38th (Welsh) Division Order No. 37. War Diary	08/09/1917	08/09/1917
Operation(al) Order(s)	C.R.E. 38th (Welsh) Division Order No. 38	10/09/1917	10/09/1917
Heading	War Diaries 38th Divisional Engineers October 1917 Vol 22		
War Diary	Croix Du Bac	01/10/1917	31/01/1918
War Diary	Croix Du Bac	22/01/1918	22/01/1918
War Diary	Merville.	01/02/1918	15/02/1918

War Diary	Steenwerck.	16/02/1918	16/02/1918
Heading	War Diaries 38 Divn R.E. March 1918 Vol 27		
War Diary	Steenwerck	01/03/1918	31/03/1918
Diagram etc	Elevation		
Miscellaneous	Schedule of principal stores-4 Raft Bridge		
Operation(al) Order(s)	C.R.E., 38th Division. Order 46	29/03/1918	29/03/1918
Operation(al) Order(s)	Table To Accompany C.R.E., 38th Division Order.46		
Heading	V. Corps. Third Army. War Diary Headquarters, Royal Engineers, 38th Division. April 1918 Attached: Operation Orders Nos. 47 to 53		
War Diary	Merville	31/03/1918	01/04/1918
War Diary	Toutencourt	02/04/1918	12/04/1918
War Diary	Contay	12/04/1918	30/04/1918
War Diary		03/04/1918	25/04/1918
Heading	Operation Orders Nos. 47 to 53		
Operation(al) Order(s)	Operation Order No. 47 38th Divisional Royal Engineers	30/03/1918	30/03/1918
Miscellaneous	Train Arrangements For Move Of 38th (Welsh) Division Less Artillery.	01/04/1918	01/04/1918
Miscellaneous	Police Arrangements.	29/03/1918	29/03/1918
Operation(al) Order(s)	Operation Order No. 48. 38th Divisional Royal Engineers. War Diary	10/04/1918	10/04/1918
Operation(al) Order(s)	Operation Order No. 49. 38th Divisional Royal Engineers.	18/04/1918	18/04/1918
Operation(al) Order(s)	38th Divisional Royal Engineers. Operation Order No. 50	21/04/1918	21/04/1918
Operation(al) Order(s)	38th Divisional Royal Engineers. Operation Order No 51	23/04/1918	23/04/1918
Operation(al) Order(s)	38th Division Royal Engineers. Operation Order No. 52	25/04/1918	25/04/1918
Operation(al) Order(s)	38th Division Royal Engineers. Operation Order No. 53	26/04/1918	26/04/1918
War Diary	Contay	01/05/1918	03/05/1918
War Diary	Toutencourt	06/05/1918	06/05/1918
War Diary	Herissart	20/05/1918	20/05/1918
Operation(al) Order(s)	38th Division Royal Engineers. Operation Order No. 54	30/04/1918	30/04/1918
Operation(al) Order(s)	38th Division, Royal Engineers. Operation Order No. 56	16/05/1918	16/05/1918
Miscellaneous	This paper cancels that issued 18th May 1918. 123rd Field Coy. R.E. and 131st Field Coy. B.E.	18/05/1918	18/05/1918
Heading	Original War Diary-June 1918 Headquarters, 38th Divisional Royal Engineers. Vol 30 1.7.1918		
War Diary	Herrisart	01/06/1918	05/06/1918
War Diary	Lealvillers	06/06/1918	29/06/1918
Operation(al) Order(s)	38th Division, Royal Engineers. Operation Order No. 59	01/06/1918	01/06/1918
Operation(al) Order(s)	Table Of Field Company Reliefs to accompany C.R.E., 38th Division, Operation Order No. 59		
Operation(al) Order(s)	38th Division, Royal Engineers, Operation Order No. 60	06/06/1918	06/06/1918
Operation(al) Order(s)	38th Division, Royal Engineers, Operation Order No. 61	20/06/1918	20/06/1918
War Diary	Lealvillers.	10/07/1918	20/07/1918
War Diary	Toutencourt	26/07/1918	31/07/1918
Heading	C.R.E. 38th Div Aug 1918		
War Diary	Toutencourt	01/08/1918	05/08/1918
War Diary	Near Lealvillers	05/08/1918	23/08/1918
War Diary	Near Hedauville	24/08/1918	24/08/1918

War Diary	Usna Redoubt.	26/08/1918	31/08/1918
Miscellaneous	C Form. Messages And Signals.		
War Diary	Messages And Signals.		
Miscellaneous	A Form. Messages And Signals		
Operation(al) Order(s)	38th Division Royal Engineers C.R.E's Operation Order No. 67	23/08/1918	23/08/1918
Operation(al) Order(s)	38th Division, Royal Engineers. Operation Order No. 68	30/08/1918	30/08/1918
Operation(al) Order(s)	Notes on C.R.E., 38th Division Op. Order No. 67	23/08/1918	23/08/1918
Operation(al) Order(s)	38th Division Royal Engineers. Operation Order No. 66	15/08/1918	15/08/1918
Miscellaneous	O.C. 124 Field Coy R.E. 38th Divn. G.S. (For information).	22/08/1918	22/08/1918
Operation(al) Order(s)	38th Division Royal Engineers C.R.E's Operation Order No. 67	23/08/1918	23/08/1918
Miscellaneous	A Form. Messages And Signals		
Miscellaneous	38th Division, G.S. 38th Division, A. & Q.	23/08/1918	23/08/1918
Miscellaneous	A Form. Messages And Signals		
Miscellaneous	38th Division, G.S. 38th Division, A. & Q.	23/08/1918	23/08/1918
Miscellaneous	38th Division, G.S. 38th Division, A. & Q. C.R.A., 38th Division.	24/08/1918	24/08/1918
Operation(al) Order(s)	38th Division, Royal Engineers. Operation Order No. 68	30/08/1918	30/08/1918
Miscellaneous	Cover for Branch Memoranda. Unregistered.		
War Diary	Usna Redoubt (W.24.b.3.7. Sheet 57.D.)	01/09/1918	01/09/1918
War Diary	Contalmaison. X.16.a.9.9. Sheet 57.D.	01/09/1918	03/09/1918
War Diary	Lesboeufs (T.4.c.O.4. Sheet 57.C)	03/09/1918	11/09/1918
War Diary	Lesboeufs (T.4.c.O.4. Sheet 57.C)	04/09/1918	05/09/1918
War Diary	Etricourt	11/09/1918	21/09/1918
War Diary	Etricourt	12/09/1918	19/09/1918
War Diary	Near Bus.	20/09/1918	28/09/1918
War Diary	Near Fins.	28/09/1918	04/10/1918
War Diary	Epehy	04/10/1918	07/10/1918
War Diary	Epehy	05/10/1918	07/10/1918
War Diary	Hindenburg Line near Vendhuille	07/10/1918	10/10/1918
War Diary	Hindenburg Line near Vendhuille	09/10/1918	09/10/1918
War Diary	Villers Outreaux	10/10/1918	11/10/1918
War Diary	Clary	11/10/1918	12/10/1918
War Diary	Bertry	12/10/1918	24/10/1918
War Diary	Bertry	12/10/1918	23/10/1918
War Diary	Montay	24/10/1918	25/10/1918
War Diary	Forest	25/10/1918	31/10/1918
Map	Part of Sheet 57B. N.E.		
Miscellaneous	C.R.E., 38th Division R.E. 5597 Report On Bridges Over River Selle On 20/10/1918	20/10/1918	20/10/1918
Diagram etc	Crib Tank Crossing Over River Selle at K.16.C.0545. Sheet 57 B.		
Miscellaneous	G.O.C.	17/10/1915	17/10/1915
Miscellaneous	Signal Arrangements For 20th	17/10/1918	17/10/1918
Diagram etc	38 Div. Communications Trunk Line Diagram. On 20.10.18		
Miscellaneous	113 Bde Sigs	19/10/1918	19/10/1918
War Diary	Forest	01/11/1918	05/11/1918
War Diary	Forest.	04/11/1918	04/11/1918
War Diary	Locquignol	05/11/1918	07/11/1918
War Diary	Berlaimont	07/11/1918	08/11/1918
War Diary	Aulnoye.	08/11/1918	26/11/1918

War Diary	Vecquemont.	01/01/1919	01/01/1919
Miscellaneous	38th Division "G". Herewith War Diaries from R.E.H.Q. and Field Companies, for February 1919	03/03/1919	03/03/1919
War Diary	Vecquemont.	01/02/1919	17/03/1919
War Diary	Vecquemont.	09/03/1919	07/06/1919

WO/95/2544/1

Commander Royal Engineers

38TH DIVISION
DIVL ENGINEERS

C. R. E.
DEC 1915 - JUN 1919

C.R.E. 38/2 Sri.
Vol I

Dec '15

Dec '15
June '19

H.Q.R.E. 38th Division.

Army Form C. 2118

Instructions regarding War Diaries and Intelligence Summaries are contained in F.S. Regs, Part II. and the Staff Manual respectively. Title Pages will be prepared in manuscript.

WAR DIARY
or
INTELLIGENCE SUMMARY
(Erase heading not required.)

December 1915

Place	Date	Hour	Summary of Events and Information	Remarks and references to Appendices
Winchester	2/12/15	8.am	HQRE left AVINGTON D Camp and embarked on transport 2108 GLENARM HEAD, and proceeded by march route to SOUTHAMPTON and the ship left at 4.15 pm. The CRE was in command of the ship which also had onboard Cyclist Company 38th Division and transport of 15th Welsh, the former under Lieut Burrell the latter under Major W R Cox	
HAVRE	3/12/15	7.am	Ship arrived at HAVRE and troops disembarked. HQRE moved from the quay at 12 noon and went to No 5 Rest Camp. The arrangement of leaving the transport parked in the road outside, and the horses in a stable inside and the men in tents halfway between the one and the other is not satisfactory entailing the unnecessary handling of blankets, rations and forage. During the afternoon the route to the entraining point was reconnoitred.	
HAVRE	4/12/15	4.30 am 7.50 1.0. 7.pm	Entrained at GARE MARITIME with H.Q. Signals and detachments of Infantry. Left the GARE MARITIME 1st Half. MESNIL BUCHY watered and fed horses. Coffee provided by French Authorities 2nd Half. ABBEVILLE. Watered and fed. Hot water available but not enough to go round all troops	
ST OMER	5/12/15	4.am 4.30. 9.0. 11.0.	arrived. an S.O. gave written instructions to HQRE. but did not have any for H.Q. Signal Co or Infantry. arrived. BLENDECQUES and detrained, during which despatch riders were sent to obtain necessary information as to site of billets & Instructions having been received HQRE proceeded by HEURINGHEM & CAUCHIE à ECQUES to CLARQUES and billeted in the farm JOVENIN. Accommodation was available for men and horses but space for CRE's office was very cramped. Orders were received to take over 46th Divisional area on 8/12/15	
CLARQUES	5/12/15		The Field Companies completed concentration and took up billets at MAMETZ.	
	6/12/15			
	7/12/15	7.45pm	Exchange of billets offered to with 46th Division cancelled.	

H.Q. R.E. 38th Division.

WAR DIARY or INTELLIGENCE SUMMARY

Army Form C. 2118

Place	Date	Hour	Summary of Events and Information	Remarks and references to Appendices
CLARQUES	8/12/15		Instructions received from Div. H.Q. all units to commence classes in Bombing, Musketry and Fieldworks. Field Companies were attached to Brigades and arrangements made for the provision of materials for Fieldworks instruction.	
	9/12/15	10.50	Instructions were received for the attachment (for instruction) of 123rd Field Company to Guards Division: from 12th to 20th December and of 124th Field Company to 19th Division.	
	10/12/15		Four officers were detailed to visit higher formations for instructional purposes during the winter viz Capt CORY Lieuts ATKINSON, WILLIS & BRAZEL of 151st, 123rd, 151st + 124th Companies respectively. CRE left for visit to C.E. XI Corps at MERVILLE. Instructions received re attachment of Field Companies to 19th Division viz 124th Co from 12th December to 5th January and another Company from 20th December to 5th January.	
	11/12/15		123rd Field Company left MAMETZ for attachment to Guards Division. 151st Company took over the general instruction of the 3 Brigades, 38th Division in Military Engineering and arranged to have an Officer available when called for, for the instruction of the Divisional Cavalry and Pioneer.	
	12/12/15		124th Field Company arrived in 19th Divisional Area and was attached to the 82nd Field Co. R.E.	
	14/12/15		151st Field Company R.E. warned to join 19th Division on 20th December and to remain till 5th January.	
	15/12/15		CRE returned from visit to CE XI Corps orders were received to send an officer to take over the School of Instruction at CALONNE SUR LYS.	

H.Q.R.E. 38th Divn.

WAR DIARY
or
INTELLIGENCE SUMMARY

Army Form C. 2118

Place	Date	Hour	Summary of Events and Information	Remarks and references to Appendices
CLARQUES	16/12/15		School at CALONNE taken over and handed to a guard of the 115th Brigade. A list of the stores taken over was forwarded to HQ 38th Divn.	
	17/12/15		Instructions were received as to the area to be occupied when moving into the Reserve area XI Corps. Orders were issued for all serviceable stores already in possession to be collected, and arrangements to be made for their subsequent removal by lorry transport.	
	18/12/15		Adjutant sent on to ST VENANT and reported that CRE's office & men in use by 46th Division would be available on their moving which was to take place on the 19th December.	
		12.30	Orders received as to the movement of the 38th Division to ST VENANT and eastwards on the 20th December. Orders received that the 123rd Field Company would return at conclusion of attachment to Guards Division direct to new billeting area.	
	19/12/15		CRE proceeded to ST VENANT and took over billets there previously occupied by 46th Division. 151st Co R.E. left MAMETZ for attachment to 81st Field Co. During the period at CLARQUES every man of HQRE fired 30 rounds rifle with 113th Infantry Brigade.	
ST. VENANT	20/12/15		HQRE left CLARQUES at 7.0 am and arrived at ST. VENANT at 2pm. no man fell out on the march 151st Fd Co reported for attachment to 81st Fd Co at Les HUITMAISONS & near by.	
	21/12/15		Ordered a party from 123rd Fd Co with an officer to be available at ST VENANT for CRE's workshop 23rd at ST VENANT for CRE's workshop Lieut ATKINSON 123rd Co R.E. ordered to report for 3 days to 151st Co R.E.	

H.Q.R.E. 38th Division.

WAR DIARY or INTELLIGENCE SUMMARY

Army Form C. 2118

Place	Date	Hour	Summary of Events and Information	Remarks and references to Appendices
ST. VENANT.	22/12/15		Arrangements were made for the hire of the timber yard of one Mme HENRI LEPOIVRE. at a rent of 20 frs per diem. Any current used for the circular saw or other machinery to be paid for by meter to the USINE ELECTRIQUE, at LILLERS.	
	23/12/15		Arrangements were made for a party of 1 N.C.O. + 15 men of the Pioneer Battalion Welsh Regiment to be attached to HQRE for loading of lorries. Arrangements were made for 5 lorries daily from 38th Divl Ammn Subpark Medical officer attached to HQRE left to join 124th Field Co. also medical cart and orderlies.	
	24/12/15		Started arrangement of drawing of bricks from HEAM DEMARLE d/BERGUETTE	
	25/12/15		Allotment of 20 wagons daily to draw bricks for 38th Division received from C.E. XIth Corps.	
	26/12/15		Instructions received for the attachment of 1 Officer and 50 other ranks to Guards Divn, and 1 Officer + 50 other ranks to 19th Division for special work on observation posts to proceed on 27th from 124th Co and 151st Co respectively. Also 1 officer + 20 other ranks from 123rd Field Co to report for the same duty to H.Q. Corps Artillery also proceeding on 27th.	
	27/12/15		Instructions received as to making of forms + tables for billets in C/Ops who CRE visited to/BERGUES steelworks in connection with possible requirements in stay in the site.	
	28/12		CRE left ST VENANT to visit trenches of 19th Division in front line	
	31/12.		CRE returned to ST VENANT. Adjutant left for instructional visit to 19th Division.	

Lewena Col. C.R.E.
38th Division.

H.Q. R.E. 38th Division.

Army Form C. 2118

WAR DIARY
or
INTELLIGENCE SUMMARY
(Erase heading not required.)

January 1916.

Instructions regarding War Diaries and Intelligence Summaries are contained in F.S. Regs., Part II. and the Staff Manual respectively. Title Pages will be prepared in manuscript.

Place	Date	Hour	Summary of Events and Information	Remarks and references to Appendices
ST VENANT	3/1/16	—	C.R.E. proceeded to H.Q. XIth Corps and took over duties of 9/CE XIth Corps. Adjutant returned from visiting CRE 19th Division.	
	16th		CRE returned from operating CE XIst Corps.	
	21st		Experiments in cutting wire with torpedos carried out by 124 Field Company at Calonne. Report forwarded to H.Q. XIst Corps.	
	24th		38th Welsh Division took over the Right section of the XIst Corps from the 19th Division.	

Eeuuum
Col.
CRE. 38th Division

<u>Confidential</u>

<u>War Diary.</u>

<u>of</u>

<u>Head quarters</u>

<u>Royal Engineers</u>

<u>38th Welsh Division</u>

<u>From</u> February 1st 1916

<u>To</u> February 29th 1916.

WAR DIARY or INTELLIGENCE SUMMARY

Army Form C. 2118

Headquarters
Royal Engineers
38th Welsh Division

February 1916

Place	Date	Hour	Summary of Events and Information	Remarks and references to Appendices
LESTREM 29 A 3.2 BETHUNE (Guidoul Sheet) EDMON 6.	1-2-16 to 4-2-16		Work in hand. General improvement of front line, joining up isolated posts, repairs to Main Street Highland Trench. Improvements to Port Arthur. Reopening Copse Street. BONO St. Communication trench. Work on Bog's Post TUBE STATION DEADCOW POST.	See Brigade Trench Maps. AREA F.6. H. LESTREM A.
	6-2-16	12.0 NOON	LIEUT C.H. BRAZEL R.E. reported for duty in relief of Capt. Adjutant.	
	7-2-16	12.0 NOON	Received orders for Capt. Adjt. G.M. MORRELL to report for duty to C.R.E. GUARDS DIVISION from C.E.XI Corps.	
	8-2-16 to 14-2-16		Work in Hand. Continued work on front line. Revetting, sandbagging, pumping & joining up isolated posts. Improvements to SIGN POST LANE HIGH LAND TRENCH, CRESCENT TRENCH, HUN STREET Trench. Improvements to PORT ARTHUR. WORK ON NORTHWESTERN RAILWAY TRAMWAY. Improvements to PLUM STREET. DRAINAGE. Reopening COPSE STREET. BOND STREET. Improvements to ST YVAST DRESSING STN. from FACTORY CORNER to RANGERS. Improvements to ROPE KEEP. ALBERTS POST. CATS POST. Continued work on DOG'S POST. TUBE STATION. ROPE KEEP. ALBERTS POST. CATS POST. Work continuing BOURNVILLE BREAST WORK. Reopening of R.O. R.E. Communication TRENCH.	
	9-2-16	12.0 NOON	CAPT G.M. MORRELL left to report to C.R.E. GUARDS DIVISION.	
	14-2-16 15-2-16 21-2-16	12.0 NOON	LIEUT C.H. BRAZEL R.E. took up entire of Adjutant. Received orders for alteration of Divisional Area (38th Div. Operation Order No 9) C.R.E. to LOCON 19th Feb. 1916. LINE EXTENDS FROM S.10 D.1 8 to GIVENCHY.	
			Work in hand. Repairs to Hun Street Curlew Street Sign Post Lane. New dug out erected New Batt. H.Q. Continued work on Port Arthur. Repairs to CORSE STREET, PLUM STREET. Reopening of BOND STREET & COCKSPUR STREET. New forks erected at RANGERS & BOARS HEAD. Work on Boys Park Rope Keep. Reopening of Pipe Communication Trench. Entrance of Bournville Breast Work. M.G. emplacement to Boars Head. at S.21. C. 8. 8. Reopening of Rope Trench.	
LOCON X.4.Central	17-2-16 18-2-16 20-2-16	6.0 p.m. 12.0 NOON 12.0 NOON	Received alteration of Operation Order No 9 (A.S.296). C.R.E. returns to LOCON 18th Feb 1916. Hand over (Brevard of Foss) to 19th Brigade moved into yard of LE TOURET X. 15. d. 8. 2. ant billets at LOCON. 33rd Div attached for instruction from QUINQUE RUE to 620 yds East of LA BASSÉE CANAL. Total line from S.10 Central to GIVENCHY. Work in hand.	
	21-2-16 28-2-16		Front line improved. Reopening of Rose Street & Cedar Street. Repairs to Crabstaff Street. Reopening of Pipe Communication trench. Work on Rope Keep. Extension of Bournville Breast Work. Work on M.G. emplacement in VILLAGE LINE. Repairs to OLD BRITISH LINE, BARNTON Communication Trench. Erection of O.P. at CANONIERS. M.G. emplacement or SIDBURY DEFENCES & WINDY CORNER DEFENCES. Repairs to NEW ROSE STREET, COVENTRY STREET, WOLFE ROAD. Erection of O.P. at GIVENCHY CHURCH. Repairs to 1500 yd WINDY CORNER & LE PLANTIN O.P.	
	22-2-16		Small amount of snow. (about 6") Drainage difficulties.	

1875 Wt. W593/826 1,000,000 4/15 J.B.C. & A. A.D.S.S./Forms/C.2118.

WAR DIARY
INTELLIGENCE SUMMARY

Army Form C. 2118

Headquarters Royal Engineers 38th Welsh Division

February 1916.

Place	Date	Hour	Summary of Events and Information	Remarks and references to Appendices
LOCON X.Y Central	26.2.16	6.0 am	Thaw became intense.	
	26.2.16	12.0 noon	Received information of Rearrangement of Fronts. (42.336 SR.D.i.). Handing over Left Brigade area (from QUINQUE RUE M S.10 D.2.8. to	See Brigade Maps AREA F.G.H Eastern A.
	28.2.16	12.0 noon	Received afternoon order. No 11 (38th Div) for handing over of Left Brigade line from QUINQUE Crossing to S.10 central.	

38th Bn.
Headquarters by
38th Division R.E.

C.R.E. 38 D
Vol 3

War Diary
of
Headquarters
Royal Engineers
38th (Welsh) Division.

From :- March 1st 1916
To :- March 31st 1916.

Army Form C. 2118

WAR DIARY
or
INTELLIGENCE SUMMARY
(Erase heading not required.)

Headquarters
Royal Engineers
38th (Welsh) Div.

Instructions regarding War Diaries and Intelligence Summaries are contained in F.S. Regs., Part II. and the Staff Manual respectively. Title Pages will be prepared in manuscript.

Place	Date	Hour	Summary of Events and Information	Remarks and references to Appendices
LOCON	1/7/16	6.00am	Resumed normal Traffic Conditions after Thaw Precautions.	
X 7 central	4/7/16	6.0pm	124th Field Coy took over Left Sector of Right Brigade from 107th Field Coy. (38 Div M O G 192)	
Between Contour Shell Earliers 6	8/7/16	6.0pm	Received instructions for Wiring of Village Line, Tuning Fork Line, Letouret Line (38 Div GS 373)	
	10/7/16		MAZINGARBE Moved to Scaled drawing Bardwire from Sailly Labourse L.3. Central. for wiring scheme. Extra Motor transport supplied by Reserve Park.	
	19/7/16	5.0pm	Test on Bangalore Torpedoes constructed in 3 length and attached sketch.	
	24/7/16		Col Achison proceeded on leave to England. Major I.W. Lamon by R.E. acting C.R.E.	
	25 to 27/7/16	11.20pm	Informed that 3 sections of 234th Field Coy 3.9 Div were to be attached for instruction on rafter 27 inst. One section to each of 123, 124, 151, Field Coys.	
	29/7/16		Received instructions for the wiring of Indian Village & Dago Post on completion of Village Line etc. (58 Div GS 472).	

Chief Engineer

    11th Corps.

REPORT OF WORK DONE UNDER C.R.E. 38th DIVISION
WEEK-ENDING 1/4/16

LEFT BRIGADE.
123 Field Co.R.E.   Continued work on M.G. emplacements in VILLAGE LINE and O.BL. Nos. 48,15,17, completed.
Work on O.P's FESTUBERT 39, CORNER HOUSE.
GIRL'S SCHOOL and BREWERY O.P's completed.
Work in OLD BRITISH LINE on traverses, dugouts parados and firesteps.
Improvements in the ISLANDS.
Wiring VILLAGE LINE.

LEFT SECTOR.
RIGHT BRIGADE.
124 Field Co.R.E.   Improvements to HITCHIN ROAD, WOLFE ROAD, HERTS AVENUE, WARE ROAD, NEW CUT, GRENADIER ROAD, NEW DOWN STREET, KINGS ROAD, PICADILLY & WINDY CORNER.
Wiring continued on VILLAGE LINE.
Work on M.G. emplacements at HERTS REDOUBT.
M.G. emplacements at GIVENCHY KEEP and FRENCH FARM completed.
Work on O.P. at FRENCH FARM.
Work on Saps B,F.H.I.J.K.

RIGHT SECTOR
RIGHT BRIGADE.
151 Field Co.R.E.   Work on O.P's SAPPER'S HOUSE, HOUSE in GIVENCHY VILLAGE. O.P. at WINDY CORNER HOUSE completed.
Work on Saps A and D. New entrance to B.
Clearing, draining and revetting ORCHARD ROAD WOLFE ROAD, HATFIELD ROAD, FINCHLEY ROAD, OXFORD TERRACE, HOPE STREET and COVENTRY STREET.
Wiring LE TOURET RESERVE LINE.
M.G. emplacements in PONT FIXE DEFENCES.

DRAINAGE COY.   Revetting and deepening SUEZ CANAL.
Revetting and widening GLAMORGAN drain
Work continued on drain E. of SUEZ CANAL by LA QUINQUE RUE

1/4/16   Lieut R.E.
                                             for C.R.E. 38th Division.

~~Chief Engineer~~
~~11th Corps.~~
War Diary

WEEKLY REPORT OF WORK UNDER C.R.E. 38th DIVISION.

FESTUBERT SECTOR

123 Field Coy R.E.
Continued work on O.P's
M.G. emplacements at LE TOURET E. and L'EPINETTE commenced.
Village LINE
Work on Islands laying trenchboards and raising parapets.
Improvements to BARNTON ROAD.
Wiring VILLAGE LINE and LE TOURET system.
O.B.L. Erecting firesteps and parados.
Work on water service from the BREWERY to RICHMOND TERRACE.
No. 5 TRAMWAY. Laying trench grids and extending Drainage.   CANADIAN ORCHARD.

GIVENCHY SECTOR.

124 and 151 Field Co. R.E.
GIVENCHY DEFENCES:-
Strutting and improvements to cellars
Work in GIVENCHY KEEP.
WINDY HOUSE O.P. completed. Work continued on other O.P's.
FRENCH FARM.   Fixing loophole plates.
COVENTRY ST.   )
WOLFE ROAD   )
ORCHARD TERRACE.)   Revetment and drainage.
HITCHEN ROAD   )
NEW CUT &   )
CALEDONIAN ROAD.)

Work on T.M. Battery dugout and PICADILLY dugout
TUNING FORK LINE.   Wiring.
Continued work on Saps.

DRAINAGE.
Work widening GLAMORGAN DRAIN (CHOCOLAT CORNER to RIVER LOISNE.)
Work on SUEZ CANAL south of MINNEHAHA RIVER
Widening at LA QUINQUE RUE.
Revetting at PONT FIXE.

25/3/16

C.R.E. 38th Division.

11th Corps.

REPORT OF WORK UNDER C.R.E. 38th DIVISION W/E 18/3/16

LEFT BRIGADE.
123 Field Co. R.E. — Continued work on M.G. emplacements in VILLAGE Line. Work on O.P. at LE PLANTIN BREWERY, CANON FARM and 39 FESTUBERT. Work in OLD BRITISH LINE erecting fire steps and parados.
Improvements in the ISLANDS.
Wiring of VILLAGE LINE.

LEFT SECTOR.
RIGHT BRIGADE.
124 Field Co. R.E. — Improvement to HITCHIN ROAD, WOLFE ROAD, QUEENS ROAD and WARE ROAD. Work on VILLAGE LINE clearing and strutting cellars. Erection of M.G. emplacements at GIVENCHY KEEP, HERTS REDOUBT and FRENCH FARM.
Work on Saps F.H.J.K.
Wire Entanglement in front of VILLAGE LINE.

RIGHT SECTOR.
RIGHT BRIGADE.
151 Field Co. R.E. — Clearing and draining ORCHARD ROAD, WOLFE ROAD, KINGS ROAD. Work extending and clearing COVENTRY STREET, GIVENCHY DEFENCES preparing site of M.G. emplacements
O.P. at WINDY HOUSE, WINDY CORNER HOUSE, and new O.P. in house in GIVENCHY VILLAGE.
Work on Saps A.Ca and D.
Wire Entanglement in LE TOURET and TUNING FORK IN LINE.

DRAINAGE CO. — Revetting of SUEZ CANAL at PONT FIXE.
Clearing drain at LA QUINQUE RUE and MENNEHAHA drain from INDIAN VILLAGE to OLD BRITISH LINE.

18/3/16

Lieut R.E.

for C.R.E. 38th Division.

Chief Engineer

11th Corps.

Weekly Report of Work done under C.R.E. 38th Division.

LEFT BRIGADE.
123rd Field Co. R.E.   SHETLAND ROAD. Reopening of trench.
                       RICHMOND TRENCH. Raising parapet and revetting.
                       BARNTON ROAD. Repairs and drainage.
                       OLD BRITISH LINE. Repairs, firesteps and parados.
                       GROUSE BUTTS. Supports and erection of   (erected.
                       ISLANDS from No 36 to the left.   breastwork.)
                            Raising of parapets and erection of traverses.
                       ISLAND No 11. Improvements.
                       Continued work on M.G. emplacements in old British
                       Line and Village Line.
                       Work on O.P. at 39 FESTUBERT, LE PLANTIN, DRESSING
                       STATION O.P. and CANON FARM.
                       Improvements to No 5 Tramway.

LEFT SECTOR
RIGHT BRIGADE
124th Field Co R.E.   HITCHEN ROAD and NEW ROAD TRENCH, repairs, revetting
                       and draining.
                       WOLFE ROAD, KINGS ROAD, QUEENS ROAD., repairs,
                       laying trenchboards and drainage.
                       VILLAGE LINE. Clearing and strutting cellars.
                       GIVENCHY KEEP. preparation of site for M.G. emplacement
                       Saps. F.H.J.K. Saps cleared and repaired.

RIGHT SECTOR
RIGHT BRIGADE
151st Field Co R.E.   Work on the following O.P.s continued.
                       WINDY CORNER HOUSE.
                       ARTILLERY HOUSE.
                       LE PLANTIN W.
                       LE PLANTIN Z.

                       GIVENCHY DEFENCES. Clearing and strutting up cellars.
                       COVENTRY STREET. Continued improvements.
                       Wiring commenced on the LE TOURET & TUNING FORK
                                                       Reserve Lines.

Drainage Company.   Continued work on SUEZ CANAL at PONT FIXE
                                                        LA QUINQUE RUE
                                                     & BARNTON ROAD.

11/3/16.   C.R.E.   38th Division.

Chief Engineer

11th Corps.

Weekly Report of work done under C.R.E. 38th Division.

LEFT BRIGADE
124rd Field Co. R.E.

Front Line improvements, raising the parapet, erecting dug-outs and traverses.
Reopening of PIPE TRENCH and repairs., clearing of COPSE STREET, BOND STREET, AND VINE STREET.
Revetting and repairs to RANGERS. Work on ROPE KEEP, erecting M.G. Emplacements.
Erection of M.G. Emplacements at :- S. 15. c. 5.3.
                                                  S. 21. b. 6.2.
                                                  S. 21. c. 5.2.
                                    n & S. 14. c. 3.8.
Repairs to LEICESTER LOUNGE O/P.

Left Brigade Area handed over to 19th Division. 1 - 3 - 16.

CENTRE BRIGADE
123rd Field Co. R.E.

Work on following O.P's   39 FESTUBERT
                                          DRESSING STATION O.P.
                                          CANON FARM.
                                          GUN HOUSE.
Work on OLD BRITISH LINE. Raising parapets, revetting and General Repairs. Raising Parapets of BARNTON ROAD. Improvements to RICHMOND TRENCH. Reopening of SHETLAND ROAD. Erection of Breastworks at the GROUSE BUTTS and raising Parapets at the ISLANDS.

RIGHT BRIGADE

GIVENCHY DEFENCES :. clearing cellars and erection of M.G. Emplacements.
FRONT LINE DEFENCES. Improvements to KINGS ROAD, QUEEN'S ROAD, WOLFE ROAD, HATFIELD ROAD ;
Raising Parapets of COVENTRY STREET.
Work on following O.P's :-
                                         WINDY HOUSE
                                         WINDY CORNER HOUSE
                                         LE PLANTIN W.
                                         LE PLANTIN Z.
                                         ARTILLERY HOUSE
                               & BELLE VIEW.

Drainage Company.   Work on SUEZ CANAL at PONT FIXE, South side of QUINQUE RUE and from CHOCOLATE MENIER CORNER to RUM CORNER.

C.R.E.   38th Division.

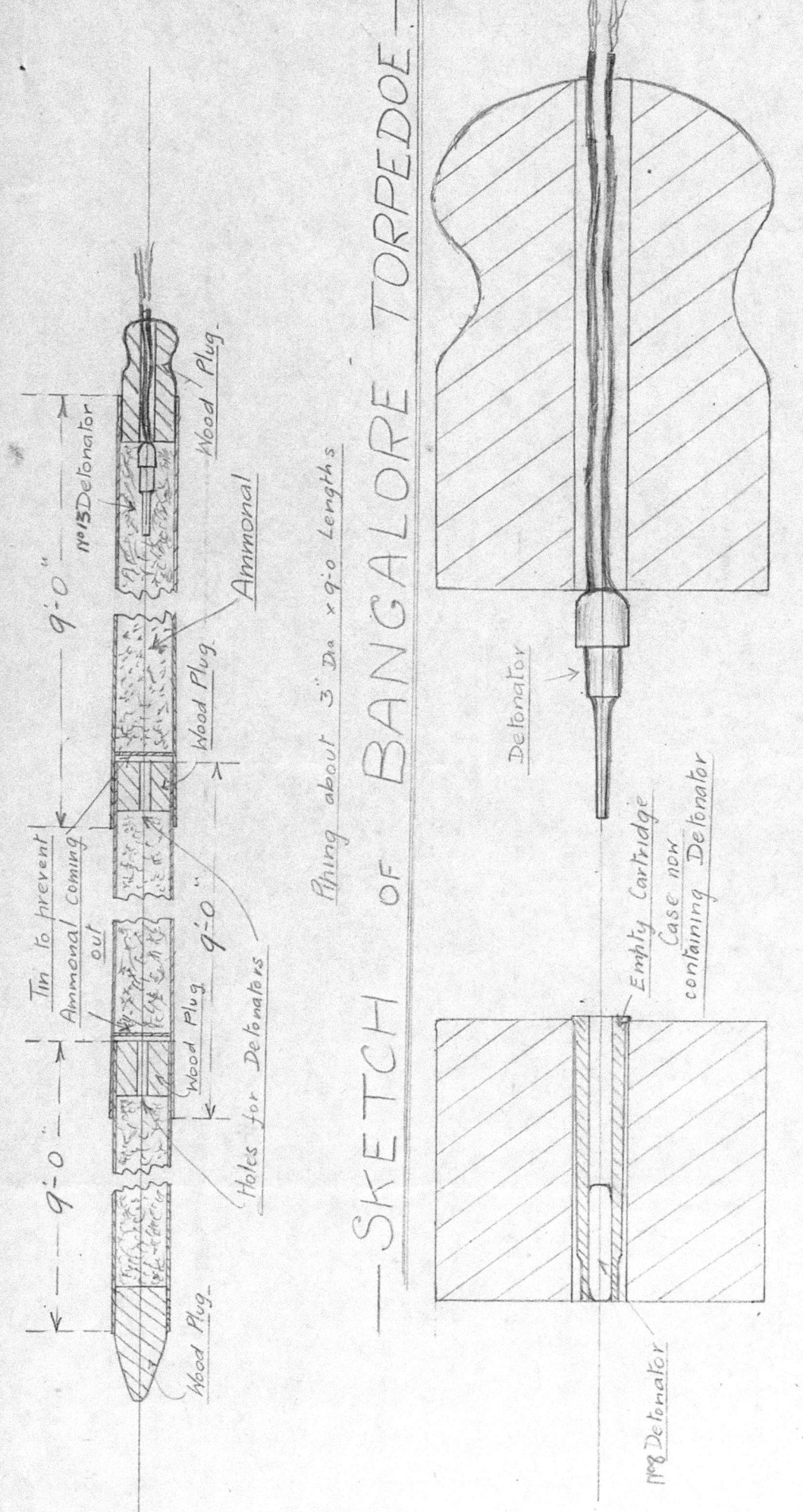

Confidential

War Diary
of
Headquarters
Royal Engineers
38th Welsh Division
for April 1916

Army Form C. 2118

WAR DIARY
or
INTELLIGENCE SUMMARY
(Erase heading not required.)

Headquarters
Royal Engineers
38th Welsh Division

Instructions regarding War Diaries and Intelligence Summaries are contained in F.S. Regs., Part II. and the Staff Manual respectively. Title Pages will be prepared in manuscript.

Place	Date	Hour	Summary of Events and Information	Remarks and references to Appendices
LOCON X 4 General Behind Combles Map (Scale)	12/7	6.0 pm	Received Operation Order No. 20 (38th Div.) for relief of 39th Div. in Givenchy & Festubert Sectors by 39th Div. and for 38th Div. taking over Hinges, Oblinghem & Vauquerreult sections from 19th & 55th Divisions.	Report to OC? Levis RE for OC 38Div.
	15/7	6.0 pm	Received Operation Order No. 21 in continuation of Operation Order No. 20. Applied to DXA for permission to be obtained from XI Corps RE for RE Stores at Nouveau Monde G27 c 38 Sheet 36A to be included in Divisional Permission granted.	
LA GORGUE 11/7 L.35 & 4-9 Sheet 36A France 3 Eastern		10.00 am	H.Q. R.E. 38th Div. moved from Locon to La Gorgue. L.35 & 4-9. Sheet 36A France 3 Eastern.	
		4.0 pm	Col. Ackman. C.R.E. 38th Div. took over RE at La Gorgue L.35 0.3.2 from 19th Division and Nouveau Monde Yard G27 c 38 from 55th Division.	

Ackman
C.R.E.
38 Division

REPORT OF WORK DONE UNDER C.R.E. 38th DIVISION
w/e 8th April 1916.

FESTUBERT SECTION
123 Field Co.R.E.

Sandbagging and concreting M.G. emplacements in VILLAGE LINE.
General Improvement of OLD BRITISH LINE.
Hurdling and revetting BARNTON ROAD and PIONEER ROAD.
Reclaiming of SHETLAND ROAD.
Work on following O.P's continued.
  34 FESTUBERT, CORNER HOUSE and CANON FARM.
ISLANDS. Considerable work revetting and raising parapets and joining up ISLANDS.
ISLAND 34 to the Left Boundary joined up.
Wiring at FESTUBERT EAST, HAYSTACK POST and DITCH KEEP.
Work on laying water pipe line from LE PLANTIN to STEWART ROAD and repairs to water pipe line from the BREWERY to RICHMOND TRENCH.

GIVENCHY SECTION.
Left Sub-sector.
124 Field Co.R.E.

Repairs, laying trenchboards and revetting in HITCHEN ROAD, HERTS AVENUE, WARE ROAD, NEW CUT, GRENADIER ROAD.
Work on HERTS REDOUBT constructing M.G. emplacements
Wiring S. of WINDY CORNER.
Wiring of VILLAGE LINE completed.
Erection of steel shelters at Batt. Headquarters.
Repair of posts and wiring in LE TOURET system.
Relaying tramway between A.13.b.10.9. and A.9.c.4.5.
SAPS. North Group. Continued work improving and extending Saps.
H. Sap blown up on 3rd instant. Continued work improving and strengthening. H Sap reopened to edge of New crater.

GIVENCHY SECTION.
Right Sub-sector.
151 Field Co.R.E.

Work on following O.P's.
  House in GIVENCHY VILLAGE and SAPPERS HOUSE.
GIVENCHY DEFENCES. Work continued at House A.15.a.4.9. and at the MAIRIE.
General repairs, laying trenchboards and revetting in COVENTRY St. WOLFE ROAD, HATFIELD ROAD, ORCHARD ROAD, OXFORD STREET, FINCHLEY ROAD and HOPE STREET.
Continued work on M.G. emplacements Nos. 4 and 16 at PONT FIXE.
Continued work on wiring of LE TOURET line.
Work on Saps C and Ca.

DRAINAGE COY.

SUEZ CANAL. at PONT FIXE, deepening and revetting.
              at LA QUINQUE RUE and RUE DE CAILLOUX
              clearing and deepening.
GLAMORGAN CANAL. Revetting and deepening.
Clearing drain between SUEZ CANAL and No. 15 ISLAND.

8/4/16

Lieut R.E.
for C.R.E. 38th Division.

~~Chief Engineer~~
~~4th Corps.~~
War Diary

REPORT OF WORK DONE UNDER C.R.E. 38th DIVISION WEEK ENDING 15/4/16.

FESTUBERT SECTION.
193rd Field Co. R.E.

M.G. Emplacements:- Work on No's 11, 15, 18 & No 5, O.B.L.

Continued work on O.P's.

Repairs to SHETLAND ROAD, PIONEER ROAD, BARNTON Rd.

Erecting Steel Shelter for ADVANCED DRESSING STATION FESTUBERT.

Continued work connecting up ISLANDS from No 30A to 37.

Work on new Water Pipe Line from Le PLANTIN TO junction of STUART ROAD AND O.B.L.

WIRING in front of O.B.L. and Festubert East.

Revetting INDIAN VILLAGE WEST.

GIVENCHY SECTION.
Left Sub-Section.
124th Field Coy. R.E.

Revetting and improving HERTS AVENUE, NEW CUT, WARE ROAD, GRENADIER ROAD & HITCHEN ROAD.

Continued work on HERTS REDOUBT, DUG-OUT for DRESSING STATION in hand.

Continued work on H & I Saps.

Repairing Posts in Le Touret System.

Relaying Tramway running from VAUXHALL BRIDGE to GIVENCHY.

GIVENCHY SECTION
Right Sub-Section
151st Field Coy. R.E.

Continued work on O.P. at Sapper's House and those in GIVENCHY Village.

Work on M.G. Emplacements in Givenchy Village and PONT FIXE DEFENCES.

Clearing and Repairing WOLFE ROAD, HATFIELD ROAD, ORCHARD ROAD and OXFORD TERR.

"FESTOONING" on Wiring in front of LE TOURET LINE.

DRAINAGE.

Widening and deepening and Revetting SUEZ CANAL, and from PONT FIXE, and SOUTH from SHETLAND ROAD.

Opening up drain from SUEZ CANAL to No 13 ISLAND.

C. Wrangel
Lieut R.E.
for C.R.E. 38th Division.

15/4/16.

~~Chief Engineer~~
 11th Corps.
War Diary

REPORT OF WORK DONE UNDER C.R.E. 38th DIVISION.

week-ending 22-4-16.

14th to 18th. Taking over FAUQUISSART and MOATED GRANGE Sections.

MOATED GRANGE SECTION.

123 Field Co. R.E.   Construction of New Batt. H.Qrs. for
                     Right and Left Batt.
                     Repairs to trolleys and track on South
                     Western Railway.
                     Concreting on No. 4 M.G. emplacements.
                     Work started on Sap near COLVIN STREET.

FAUQUISSART SECTION.

124 and 151 Field Co. R.E.   Reclaiming front line near RED LAMP
                             SALIENT.
                             RIFLEMANS TRENCH, ROTTEN ROW, BOND
                             STREET, 300 YARDS TRENCH, Nth ELGIN
                             STREET, Sth ELGIN STREET, MASSELOT St,
                             DRURY LANE, FLEET STREET.
                             Clearing trenches, revetting and
                             laying trenchboards.
                             Improvements to following posts.
                             DEAD END POST, COPSE POST, HAUGOMONT
                             POST, WANGERIE POST, ROAD END POST,
                             FORT D'ESQUIN, FIREWORKS POST,
                             MASSELOT POST, MASSELOT HOUSE.

22-4-16   C H Brazel Lieut R.E.

                                         for C.R.E. 38th Division.

~~Chief Engineer~~
~~K1th Corps.~~
War Diary

WEEKLY REPORT OF WORK DONE UNDER C.R.E. 38th Division
w/e 29-4-16.

MOATED GRANGE SECTION.
123 Field Co. R.E.   Construction of New Right and Left Batt. H.Qrs.
                     Work on Support Line near Grants Post and
                     Sth. TILLELOY STREET.
                     Improvements on ERITH ROAD.
                     Wiring on WINCHESTER POST.
                     Repairs to trolleys and line on STH. EASTERN
                     Drainage of RESERVE LINE.   RAILWAY.
                     Continued Sapping at COLVIN STREET.
                     Erection of Anti-Gas doorways at WINCHESTER
                     POST Medical Inspection Post.

FAUQUISSART SECTION.
124 and 151 Field Coys. Erection of O.P's.
                     Work on THE PEAK, CHAPIGNY CHIMNEY completed.
                     Extension of CONVENT O.P.
                     Work on BRISTOL and TEA HOUSE O.P's.
                     Commenced new O.P. next to BERKELEY.
                     Repairs to C.R.A's HOUSE.
                     Repairs and revetting N. and S. ELGIN STREET,
                     DRURY LANE and FLEET STREET.
                     Work on FAUQUISSART POST erecting Bomb Store,
                     and repairs to ELGIN POST ROAD BEND and
                     WANGERIE.
                     Work on 300 YARDS TRENCH and RIFLEMANS TRENCH
                     ROTTEN ROW and SOUTHERNDOWN AVENUE.
                     Repairs to MIDLAND RAILWAY.

29-4-16.
                                              Lieut R.E.
                                       for C.R.E. 38th Division.

RE 38/5 Vol 1

Confidential

War Diary.

Headquarters

Royal Engineers

38th Welsh Division

May 1916

WAR DIARY Army Form C. 2118
or
INTELLIGENCE SUMMARY
(Erase heading not required.)

Headquarters
Royal Engineers
38th Welsh Div.
May 1916

Place	Date	Hour	Summary of Events and Information	Remarks and references to Appendices
LA GORGUE L35 b1.9 Sheet 36 a/b France EDITION 5	14/5/16		Received 1st Army Letter R/1/960 appointing Col E.H.de V. Atkinson as CE 1st Corps & to be Brig General and Major G.S. Knox to be Corps to be Lt Colonel & C.R.E. 38th Div vice Col Atkinson.	
	16/5/16	12 noon	Lt Col Knox assumed to take up duty.	
	19/5/16		Brig Gen Atkinson K.H.S.O to take up duty as C.E. 1st Corps.	
	26/5/16		Received 38 Div letter GS 9/2/1 dated 26.5.16 re attachment of 61st Div for instruction. 1 Field Coy details 3rd Div R.E. to commence on 3/6/16.	
	31/5/16		158 Officers & men from 61st Division report for instruction with 123rd & 124th & 151st Field Coys R.E.	Summary of work carried out by R.E. 38th Division in month is attached.

E. Shewan
C.R.E.,
38th (Welsh) Division.

Chief Engineer
War Diary
XIth Corps.

WEEKLY REPORT OF WORK DONE UNDER C.R.E. 38th DIVISION.

MOATED GRANGE SECTION.
123 Field Co. R.E.   M.G. emplacements.
<u>Front Line</u>. Preparing foundations for Nos 3 and 3a.
MOATED GRANGE. Concrete work on No. 4.
BACQUEROT LINE. Work on No. B and B2. M.G.E.
<u>COLVIN SAPS</u>. OLD COLVIN Sap completed into crater. Continued work joining New Sap with Old.
WINCHESTER POST)
MIN POST.   ) Wiring.
Work on WINCHESTER Comm. Trench.
         BIRDCAGE WALK
         SOUTH TILLELOY STREET.
New RIGHT BATT. HEADQUARTERS completed.
New LEFT BATT. HEADQUARTERS. Good progress made.
Hop Screen planted to screen EPINETTE Emergency Roads.

FAUQUISSART SECTION.
124 and 151 Field Coys.   <u>FRONT LINE</u>. General repairs - erecting fire-steps, and refixing trenchboards.
Repairs to M.G. emplacements and dugouts.
Continued work on CHORD behind RED LAMP SALIENT.
Work on North and South ELGIN STREET, Drury LANE, MASSELOT, FLEET STREET, RIFLEMANS AVENUE.
<u>PICADILLY, GREAT NORTH ROAD.</u> Revetting and raising of parapets.
Continued work on BACQUEROT LINE.
Relaying MIDLAND RAILWAY track.
<u>Work on following POSTS.</u>
LAVENTIE, PICANTIN, JOCKS LODGE, A 1 Flank, HOUGAMONT, DEAD-END, COPSE, MASSELOT.
<u>Work on following O.P's.</u>
THE PEAK, DEAD COW, C.R.A. HOUSE, CONVENT, SNOWDOWN, FARM O.P., COTTAGE, TEA SHOP.

<u>SCREENING.</u> Cutting and planting willow wands to screen RUE TILLELOY.

6-5-16.

Lieut R.E.
for C.R.E. 38th Division.

Chief Engineer
War Diary
14th Corps.

PROGRESS REPORT OF WORK DONE UNDER C.R.E.38th Div.

MOATED GRANGE SECTION
123 Field Co. R.E.
M.G. Emplacements. Concreting work on Nos. 2S and 2.
in Front Line, Nos. 5 and 6 in ROUGE CROIX and No.4
MOATED GRANGE.
Work continued screening RUE TILLELOY and RUE
BACQUEROT.
Reclaiming WINCHESTER Trench.
ANNETTE Emergency Roads. Continued bridging ditches.
Continued work on COLVIN Saps.
Work on TILLELOY, GRANTS POST, WIN POST and LONELY
SMITH continued.
Repairs to Pump at PUMP HOUSE.
Relaying BACQUEROT Railway.

FAUQUISSART SECTION.
124 and 151 Field Co. Work on following O.P's.
PEAK, DEAD COW, C.R.A. HOUSE, SNOWDOWN, FARM, COTTAGE
BERKLEY, CONVENT. PEA SHOP O.P. completed.
Relaying MIDLAND RAILWAY track.
General repairs in Front Line.
Screening RUE TILLELOY.
Wiring BACQUEROT Line.
Wiring continued on MASSELOT and HOUGOUMONT.
Work on communication trenches, 300 YARDS TRENCH,
PICADILLY, N. and S. ELGIN STREET and DRURY LANE.

13/5/16

Chief Engineer
XIth Corps. *War Diary*

PROGRESS REPORT OF WORK DONE UNDER C.R.E. 38th DIVISION
w/e 20-5-16.

MOATED GRANGE SECTION
123 Field Co.R.E.

M.G. Emplacements
Concreting work on Nos 23 and 24 FRONT LINE, MOATED GRANGE Nos 5 and 6 ROUGE CROIX, No. 4 WINCHESTER POST and No. 3 LONELY POST.

Work on Trench Tramways at Railhead.
RUGBY POST Wiring completed.
Revetting Reserve Line at LONELY, ERITH and GRANTS POST.
Drainage of New Reserve Line in hand.
Construction of Trench Mortar Emplacements
Steel dugouts for Bomb Stores at ROUGE CROIX and EPINETTE.

FAUQUISSART SECTION.
124 and 151 Field Co.R.E.

Work on following O.P's.
PEAK, C.R.A's HOUSE, CONVENT, SNOWDON, FARM, COTTAGE, MOATED GRANGE, CASTLE CRICCIETH, and BERKLEY.
Relaying GREAT NORTHERN RAILWAY and MIDLAND RAILWAY tracks.

General Repairs to Front Line.
Work on Communication Trenches, RIFLEMANS AVENUE, PICADDILY, MASSELOT, DRURY LANE, NORTH and SOUTH ELGIN STREET.

Screening of ROAD BEND to WANGERIE.

Wiring RUE BACQUEROT LINE.

Work on M.G.E's in MASSELOT POST.

Wiring between DEAD END and PICANTIN.

(sgd) J.E. HARBEN 2/Lt R.E

Chief Engineer
~~War Diary~~
~~XIth Corps.~~

WEEKLY PROGRESS OF WORK DONE UNDER C.R.E. 38th DIVISION
w/e 27 - 5 - 16.

MOATED GRANGE SECTION.　　　Good progress made on the following
123 Field Co. R.E.　　　　　M.G.E's:- No. 30 Front Line, No. 4
　　　　　　　　　　　　　　MOATED GRANGE, Nos 5 and 6 ROUGE CROIX
　　　　　　　　　　　　　　No. 3 WINCHESTER, No. 5 LONELY.
　　　　　　　　　　　　　　RESERVE LINE. Work on DREADNOUGHT POST,
　　　　　　　　　　　　　　BIRDCAGE WALK.
　　　　　　　　　　　　　　Extension of BACQUEROT RAILWAY, and
　　　　　　　　　　　　　　fixing trench grids.
　　　　　　　　　　　　　　Erection of Bomb Stores at LA BASSEE
　　　　　　　　　　　　　　and L'EPINETTE Dumps.
　　　　　　　　　　　　　　Wiring nearly completed near MON POST.

FAUQUISSART SECTION.
124 and 151 Field Co.R.E.　Relaying track on MIDLAND RAILWAY.
　　　　　　　　　　　　　　Revetting and sandbagging MASSELOT
　　　　　　　　　　　　　　Communication Trench.
　　　　　　　　　　　　　　Construction of MASSELOT M.G.E's.
　　　　　　　　　　　　　　Wiring BACQUEROT LINE.
　　　　　　　　　　　　　　TRAMWAYS. GT. NORTHERN and GT.CENTRAL
　　　　　　　　　　　　　　Repairs to trolleys and track.
　　　　　　　　　　　　　　POSTS. Wiring between DEAD END and
　　　　　　　　　　　　　　PICANTIN POSTS. Excavation for M.G.E's
　　　　　　　　　　　　　　Nos. 10, 11, 12 and 14.
　　　　　　　　　　　　　　O.P's Brickwork continued in towers of
　　　　　　　　　　　　　　CONVENT, SNOWDON, PAIGN and COTTAGE O.P's
　　　　　　　　　　　　　　Strutting of C.R.A's House.
　　　　　　　　　　　　　　Work continued on MOATED GRANGE, PEAK,
　　　　　　　　　　　　　　CASTLE CRICCIETH and MIN O.P's.
　　　　　　　　　　　　　　FRONT LINE. Work on RED LAMP SALIENT,
　　　　　　　　　　　　　　T.M.E's and general repairs to fire-
　　　　　　　　　　　　　　steps, parados and parapet.

　　　　　　　　　　　　　　　　　　　　　　　　2/Lieut R.E.
27-5-16　　　　　　　　　　　for C.R.E. 38th Division.

R.E. 38/3 Vol 6

Headquarters Royal Engineers
38th Welsh Division

War Diary
for
June 1916.

Confidential

Army Form C. 2118

WAR DIARY
or
INTELLIGENCE SUMMARY
(Erase heading not required.)

Headquarters
Royal Engineers
38th Welsh Division
April 1918

Instructions regarding War Diaries and Intelligence Summaries are contained in F.S. Regs., Part II. and the Staff Manual respectively. Title Pages will be prepared in manuscript.

Place	Date	Hour	Summary of Events and Information	Remarks and references to Appendices
La Gorgue 35b7.9 sheet 36A Sh 3	10/4	9.0am	Received 38th Div. Order No. 29 re Relief of 50th Div. by 61st Div. on Divisional and Corps Fronts (Scheme after name Rippuls). Headquarters to Gare La Gorgue 20 rooms on 12 June.	
		6.0pm	All attached Infantry Pioneers & R.E. attached at G.H.Q. Lines placed to rescue units, with exception of one Coy. 1/4th / Glo. & Suffolks, who are already moved. Arrival of C.R.E. 61 Div. to arrange taking over.	
	11/6	12 noon	In Jan of 12am 1/4 Suff. Bn returned to a' Buones by motor Lorry.	
		1-0pm	Received 38 Div Order No 29 to move from La Gorgue to St Venant on 12th inst.	
	12/6	10.0 am	R.E. Headquarters left La Gorgue for St Venant via Merville, conveyed by two motor lorries. Arrived St Venant 11.30am.	
	13/6	6.0pm	Received 38th Div Order to move to St Michel on 13th inst.	
St Venant D.H.Q.	13/6	9.30am	Left St Venant for St Michel (F.13.c.05) sheet 36B arrived 12.30pm	

Manuel?
Maj. R.E.
Act. C.R.E. 38th Div. Div.

WAR DIARY
or
INTELLIGENCE SUMMARY
(Erase heading not required.)

Army Form C. 2118

Headquarters
Royal Engineers
38th Welsh Division
June 1916.

Place	Date	Hour	Summary of Events and Information	Remarks and references to Appendices
MICHEL	19/6		C.R.E. Lt Col KNOX proceeded on leave to England.	
13 C.O.S tance w/ 36b	16th TO 24th 23/6		Drawing of 2nd Div Corps on Training Scheme at Mackey Breton	
			Received 38 Div Order N° 31/6 from R Rubrancourt on 26th inst. Divisional Exercise. 38th Div Corps & Pioneers under command of C.R.E. They advance to encounter Germans (?) hid in rear of Reum Bee. Reconnaissance Patrols of 1 Officer + 4 Other Ranks reported to overcome Brig who is to report on necessary works for employment of captured ground. (H.Q.H.L.) Lt Michel at 3.45 p.m.	
13RAO COURT	26th			
	27th		Received 38 Div Order N° 32 to proceed to Rubimbré, arriving 6.30 p.m.	
uls S.W. of ERNAVILLE END MAP.	23rd	4-0 p.m.	Received 38 Div H.Q. G 627 cancelling 38 Div Order N° 32. Lt Col KNOX returned from leave.	
	30th		Received 38 Div Order N° 33 to proceed to Rubempré on 30th inst. Ins pecking of Div Corps by C.E. 2nd Corps. Left Rubrancourt at 11.45 p.m. arrived Rubempré (T.13.b.7.1.3 Ruk g/t at midnight.	

S Kennedy
Maj RE
a/c. C.R.E.
38th Div.

Confidential

Vol 4

War Diary
of
Headquarters
Royal Engineers
38th Welsh Div

July 1916

WAR DIARY
or
INTELLIGENCE SUMMARY

(Erase heading not required.)

Army Form C. 2118

Headquarters
Royal Engineers
38th Welsh Division
July 1916

Place	Date	Hour	Summary of Events and Information	Remarks and references to Appendices
RUBEMPRÉ (T.13.B.7.1.)	1/7	9.0 am	Arrived Rubempré (T.13.B.7.1.) at midnight (31.20.1.5). Lt Col G.S. KNOX admitted to Hospital suffering from injuries received on night 30th June by being thrown from his horse.	
13.B.7.1. Hut 57 D (FRANCE)		5.25 pm	Received 38th Div wire G.17 "All units to be in readiness to move at 7.0 hrs."	
TOUTENCOURT I central Hut 57 D (FRANCE)	3/7	8.15 pm	Moved to Billets in TOUTENCOURT (U.1.D.9.9) at 3.45 pm. Arrived 9.45 pm.	
		3.15 pm	Received orders for Officer in charge reports to receive orders for move.	
		4.15 pm	Received orders to proceed to MERICOURT L'ABBÉ (J.3.D.5. Sht. 62 D FRANCE). via Contay (FRANVILLERS, HEILLY, HEILLY-HAUTE). Left Toutencourt 8.30 pm.	
MERICOURT L'ABBÉ & D Sht 62 D (FRANCE)	4/7/16	12.30 am	Arrived 12.30 am. Men went bivouacing.	
	5/7	Midday	Received 38th Div message G.129 re relief of 7th Div by 38 Div on night 5th–6th. Received 38 Div Orders No 35 to relieve 7th Div holding line North of MAMETZ from X.23.c.4.6 to X.23.d.2.6. X.29.b.5.5. to S.25.b.0.1. (ref MONTAUBAN TRENCH MAP). 17 Div left 19th Div on Right. Arrived GROVETOWN CAMP 6.0 pm.	
GROVETOWN CAMP I central Sht "Albert" (central) (France)	6/7/16	12.0 noon	Lt Col R.G. FALCON arrived to take up duty as Chief Engineer vice Lt Col G.S. KNOX admitted to hospital on 1/7.	
		9.0 pm	Received 38th Div Order No 36 re attack on MAMETZ WOOD at 8.0 am on 7th in conjunction with 17th Div on the left.	

Army Form C. 2118

WAR DIARY
or
INTELLIGENCE SUMMARY
(Erase heading not required.)

Headquarters R.E.
38th Welsh Division
July 1916

Instructions regarding War Diaries and Intelligence Summaries are contained in F. S. Regs., Part II. and the Staff Manual respectively. Title Pages will be prepared in manuscript.

Place	Date	Hour	Summary of Events and Information	Remarks and references to Appendices
	7/7/16	9.5 pm	Received 38th Div. Order No G 360 re raid on Strip trench by 113 Inf. Bde.	
	8/7/16	11.40 pm	Received 38th Div. Order No 37 re attack on Mametz Wood by 115 Inf. Bde at 2-0 am on 9th inst.	
	9/7/16	2.0 am	Received 38th Div. Order No 38 re attack on Mametz Wood at 4-0 am. This attack was postponed until 4-0 am on 10th inst.	See detailed account on appendices
		9.45 pm	Received 38th Div. Order No 39 re attack on Mametz Wood at 4-0 am on 10th inst by 113 & 114 Inf. Bdes.	

Army Form C. 2118

WAR DIARY
or
INTELLIGENCE SUMMARY
(Erase heading not required.)

Headquarters Royal Engineers 38th Welsh Div
July 1916

Instructions regarding War Diaries and Intelligence Summaries are contained in F.S. Regs., Part II. and the Staff Manual respectively. Title Pages will be prepared in manuscript.

Place	Date	Hour	Summary of Events and Information	Remarks and references to Appendices
GROVETOWN CAMP	11/7/16	12 noon	Received Orders to proceed to TREUX (J & 6. ALBERT COMBINED SHEET). Leaving Amientown Camp 5-30pm	
		7-30pm	Arrived @ TREUX	
TREUX J & 6 ALBERT COMBINED SHEET	12/7/16	9-0am	Received Orders to entrain at "EDGE HILL" station (E.19 a Acurate Combined sheet) at 6-0 p.m.	
		7-30	Left Edge Hill station.	
	13/7/16	2-0am	Arrived @ LONG PRÉ (10 miles S.E. of ABBEVILLE) proceeded to 38th D.H.Q. at PONT REMY (4½ miles SE of ABBEVILLE) arriving at 3-0 a.m.	
PONT REMY		9-0am	Received orders to proceed by Motor Bus to RUSEMPRÉ (T.13 & 14 54D FRANCE).	
		2-30pm	Left PONT REMY. to join Column at Longpré	
		7-30pm	Column of 15 Buses left Longpré	
		11-0pm	Arrived RUSEMPRÉ	
RUSEMPRE	14/7/16	7-30	Received Orders to proceed COUIN (J.I. & 14 54D France)	
		1-0pm	Left Rusempré 1-0 p.m.	
		6-0pm	Arrived COUIN. Received orders re taking of line from 48th Div. Relief of R.E. Coys started on night of 14th.	
COUIN	15/7/16		Took over from 48 Div the line from K.17.A.2.7½. to K.35.A.6.9. RE as unfurler Couecures J.3.c.5.8. Courcelles, J.29.c.9.5, The Bucc J.23.a.8.8.	See attached account as appendix

1875 Wt. W593/826 1,000,000 4/15 J.B.C.&A. A.D.S.S./Forms/C.2118.

WAR DIARY

Army Form C. 2118

Headquarters Royal Engineers 38th Welsh Div.
July 1916

Place	Date	Hour	Summary of Events and Information	Remarks and references to Appendices
COUIN (J.1) (Rue 57 D)	23/7	6-0 pm	Received 38 Div Order No 47 re relief of 36th Ulster Div by 113th Inf Bde 38th Div. New Right Div Boundary Q.4 b 76.75.	
	26/7	11-30 pm	Received 38th Div Order No 48 re relief of 38th Div by 20th Div on 28th & 29th inst.	
	28th	Noon	Handed over to C.R.E. 20th Div.	
	29th	11-0 pm	Received 38th Div Order No 49 re entrainment of Troops at Doullens & Candas on 30 & 31st.	
		10-0 am	HQ RE moved from COUIN to BUS (J26) (Hut 57 a.)	
		11-0 am	Issued C.R.E. Order No 12 re entrainment of HQ RE & Field Coys.	
BUS J26 Hut 54 (a)	30th	11-20 pm	HQ RE left Bus for Doullens for entrainment.	
	31st	4-30 am	(123 Div'l Coy on same train)	
		6-19 am	Rfd Douellens for Hazebrouck	

Army Form C. 2118

WAR DIARY
or
INTELLIGENCE SUMMARY

H.Q. R.E. 38th Welsh Div
July 1916

(Erase heading not required.)

Instructions regarding War Diaries and Intelligence Summaries are contained in F. S. Regs., Part II. and the Staff Manual respectively. Title Pages will be prepared in manuscript.

Place	Date	Hour	Summary of Events and Information	Remarks and references to Appendices
~~Boeschepe~~ ~~Abeele STN~~	3/7	11.00am	Arrived Hazebrouck & remainder entrained to Proceed to Prop. HOPOUTRE STN (South W/ Poperinghe) (L 17 & 68.) Sheet 27	
POPERINGHE BELGIUM.		12.15pm	Arrived HOPOUTRE* - detrained. Received instructions to proceed to Esquelbecq	
		2.0pm	Left HOPOUTRE Stn. & proceeded to Esquelbecq via Abeele. NATO v. HOUTKERQUE, HERZEELE, WORMHOUDT.	
ESQUELBECQ. Sheet 27		7.30pm	Arrived & Billets at ESQUELBECQ.	

Napoleon
Lt. Col.
C.R.E.
38th Welsh Div

REPORT BY C.R.E. 38TH DIVISION ON OPERATIONS BETWEEN
JULY 5TH and 15TH 1916.

Reference MONTAUBAN Trench Map and attached

5th July. Major I.W. LAMONBY a/C.R.E. and Lt.Col. BOILEAU C.R.E.
7th Division present.
8 pm. The C.R.E. and 19th Welsh (Pioneer) Regiment arrived
at GROVETOWN - 123 Field Co. R.E. at WATERLOO JUNCTION -
124 Field Co. R.E. at HALTE - 151 Field Co. R.E. at
MINDEN POST.
8-45 pm. O.C. 124 Field Co. R.E. ordered to report to G.O.C.
113 Brigade to make strong points in WOOD TRENCH, if
captured, at X.24.c.0.7. and X.24.d.4.6.. He sent
No. 1 and No. 2 Sections.

6th July
2-30 am These Sections arrived at VALLEY TRENCH at 2-30 am but
were not required so returned to the HALTE.
The Officers of this Company reconnoitred during the
day and drew out schemes for consolidating. These
were not carried out as the 17th Division took over
our Left.
123 Field Company was in Reserve at WATERLOO JUNCTION
all day.
151 Field Company, less 1 and 2 Sections, were employed
in taking material to the LOOP with 6 A.S.C. wagons.
Lt. Col. C.G. FALCON took over duties of C.R.E at 2 pm.

7th July.
1-10 am Ordered (A.1.) O.C. 151 Field Company to report to
headquarters 115 Brigade who were to attack the east-
ern portion of MAMETZ WOOD at 8-30 am - One Company
of 19th (Welsh) Pioneers were attached to them. Their
work to consist of making Strong Points at X, 8.18.b.90.75.
C and B.
Nos. 1 and 2 Sections 151 Field Company had already
proceeded to CATERPILLAR WOOD RAVINE arriving 3 am.
They prepared the North edge of the RAVINE for defence
and made a communication trench across it. They returned at 8 pm. Nos. 3 and 4 Sections of the Pioneer
Company remained at the LOOP until ordered forward
at 4 pm. by G.O.C. 115 Brigade to the RAVINE. The
attack timed for 5-30 pm was postponed and the R.E.
and Pioneers were withdrawn.
At 4-10 pm, as these expeditions had not been reported
to C.R.E. the 151 Field Company and 1 Company Pioneers
were ordered (A.12) to put CATERPILLAR WOOD and
MARLBOROUGH WOOD in a state of defence, commencing
when dusk. This order did not reach them in time.
123 Field Company remained all day at MINDEN POST in the rain
124   "   "   "   "   "   "   " HALTE   "   "   "
At 4-10 pm (A.14) 123 Field Company were ordered to
return to bivouac and (A.15) 124 Field Company to have
one section ready to consolidate the neck of the wood
at X.24.c.1.1. if captured in the evening by the 113
Brigade, the remainder to return to their bivouac. The
Pioneers (A.15) were ordered to detail one company to work
with 151 Field Company and 2 Companies to dig a communication trench from X.29.b.5.5. to X.30.a.0.7. if the
neck of the wood was captured.

- 2 -

8th July. 151 Field Company ordered (A.19) to carry out at dusk the work ordered for previous night when the order was received too late. At 3-35 pm 151 Field Company and 1 company Pioneers ordered (A.22) to report to Headquarters 114 Brigade with regard to this work. The work carried out consisted of wiring, bombing stop, straightening old German trench for defence by Lewis Gun, 2 Machine Gun Emplacements and communication trenches.

123 Field Company formed a dump at QUEENS NULLAH, repaired heavy bridges and made a foot road to POMMIER REDOUBT.

124 Field Company, No. 4 Section with 220 Infantry carrying material to QUEENS NULLAH.

At 5-0 pm ordered 124 Field Company (A.26) to report to 113 Brigade to be ready to make strong points if the South end of the wood was captured in the attack ordered for 2 am 9-7-16. Three points near X.24.c. central and one at junction of WOOD TRENCH and STRIP TRENCH.

Two companies of Pioneers detailed for digging communication trench from CLIFF TRENCH to STRIP TRENCH.

One company of Pioneers to improve the road through MAMETZ.

9th July 123 Field Company continued to take stores with Infantry carrying parties of 100 to QUEENS NULLAH and party of 178 to CATERPILLAR WOOD during the past night, and with 100 Infantry to POMMIER REDOUBT during the day. The foot roads from HALTE and MINDEN POST to POMMIER REDOUBT were improved.

151 Field Company were withdrawn from CATERPILLAR at dawn to MINDEN POST.

124 Field Company, less No. 4 Section, under orders of 113 Brigade went to QUEENS NULLAH at 12-5 am. to await the attack which was not launched. After waiting under heavy shell fire till 4 am they were withdrawn to the HALTE but were shelled out and moved to MINDEN POST (1 killed).

At 9 pm. orders (A.37) were sent to 123 Field Company to be at QUEENS NULLAH at 3 am. on the 10th in order to carry out two special lines of wiring across the wood N, O, X, and P.U.V. with 200 yards flanking wire at P and X. - to receive orders from 113 Brigade when the Wood had been captured. Order sent by Headquarters 38th Division to 113 Brigade that the 123 Field Company was not to be sent into the wood until the Infantry had reached the line XYOKN.

10th July 123 Field Company rendezvous was changed to SHRINE ALLEY behind MAMETZ and they reached it at 2-40 am and reported to 113 Brigade at DANTZIG ALLEY at 3-0 am. The Brigade attacked at 4-15 am. At 6-40 am Nos 1 and 4 sections sent to QUEENS NULLAH, followed at 7-5 am by the other 2 sections. At 7-15 am 2/Lieuts. MACLEAN and LETHBRIDGE sent to reconnoitre line and told if favourable to wire it immediately and after Major LAMONBY had inspected it he ordered Nos. 1 and 4 sections at 8-15 am to commence work. This work was along the cross road and was not one of the special objects the Company had been ordered to carry out. Nos 1 and 4 sections were relieved by Nos. 2 and 6 sections at 11-45 am.

Major LAMONBY took command of the left of the attack from 8-30 to 9-30 am. No Infantry Officers being left.

The 113 Brigade made a further attack at 4-15 pm

The Right got within 200 yards of the top of the wood but the Left only got to the Railway and consolidated at J. The 124 Field Company and Pioneers meanwhile held the line of the bottom cross roads.
5-30 to 7-0 pm No. 3 Section made a Strong Point at Y.

For all this work the 124 Field Company had been placed at the disposal of the 113 Brigade and if they had been employed by the Brigadier on R.E. Work only, they would have been sufficient to do it. 123 Field Company could then have been kept in Reserve and fresh and ready to do the particular wiring work which was considered by the Division to be of great importance not in the capture of the wood but for holding it against heavy counter-attacks.

124 Field Company, under orders from 113 Brigade, sent Nos 2 and 3 Sections with 1½ Companies 19th (Welsh) Pioneers to a position behind DANTZIG ALLEY and No. 1 section and ½ Company Pioneers to QUEENS NULLAH at 3 am.

At 5-45 am the South edge of the wood was reported clear so No. 1 Section and ½ Company Pioneers were sent to make Strong Point at junction of WOOD TRENCH and WHITE TRENCH which they completed by 6 pm.

At 6 am No. 2 and 3 Sections ordered to QUEENS NULLAH and G.O.C. 113 Brigade ordered the 1½ Company Pioneers to go to the HALTE to bring up ammunition.

At 7-45 am Nos. 2 and 3 Sections started a Strong Point at the bottom cross roads and the Pioneers made a trench from CLIFF trench to STRIP trench.

Major KIRKWOOD was put in command of the left of the line by Col. GOSSETT 4th Army Staff from 8-0 to 8-30 am.

At 9 am as the Infantry were not making sufficient progress with their trench at the first cross road, 1½ Company Pioneers were brought up.

At 4-15 pm. the R.E. and Pioneers held the trench during the forward attack - and during the night.

At. 6 pm No. 1 section was sent to QUEENS NULLAH and at 7 pm to MINDEN POST.

151 Field Company at the disposal of the 114 Brigade on the Right was ordered to send No. 1 section under Sergeant J.S. CLARKE with 1 Company (less 1 platoon) Pioneers to rendezvous and form a dump near the junction of BEETLE ALLEY and WHITE TRENCH at 3 am.

The remainder of the Company with the 19th (Welsh) Pioneers (less 2 Companies and 3 platoons) went to CATERPILLAR WOOD RAVINE at the same hour
At 4-45 am half No. 1 section and 1 platoon Pioneers were sent to make a strong point at X.24.a.7.2., the other half section with another platoon to make a strong point near the bottom cross roads. The work was completed by 2 pm. and the men were ordered by the Senior Infantry Officer present to garrison the posts.

At 8-45 am Nos. 2 and 3 sections each accompanied by one platoon Pioneers, were sent to make strong points at A, C and X. Owing to Machine Gun fire they were unable to get up the ravine so they went over the spur due west.

As X was not captured the party for it was sent back to help at A and C. The work was completed by 2 pm and the sections returned to MINDEN by QUEENS NULLAH.

No. 1 section and the remainder of the 19th (Welsh) Pioneers attempted to form a communication trench along the ravine from CATERPILLAR to MAMETZ WOOD - As they had many casualties in the first minute from Machine Gun fire they started to sap it. Owing to

- 4 -

to the lie of the ground this proved to be impracticable - it would probably have been better to have worked straight over the spur due west. At 10 pm. messengers were sent to tell them to withdraw. The Pioneers were found but the messages were not delivered to No. 1 section.

11th July

The 114 Brigade were relieved by the 115 Brigade and at 10 am Nos. 2, 3, and 4 sections were ordered from MINDEN to POMMIER REDOUBT and at 1 pm. they were ordered to MAMETZ WOOD to make three Strong Points East of the central ride as soon as the Infantry had captured it.

At 3-30 the attack started but was not successful and at 10 pm. the R.E. were ordered to withdraw.

At 3 am. 123 Field Company had rations brought up by a party of No. 4 section when the O.C. sent for all men available from the bivouac (cooks, Headquarters Section etc.) and obtained 32 men.

At 7 am No. 3 section ordered to wire line V.W.X., they were reinforced by the 32 men and completed the work by 11 am.

At 8-45 am No. 2 section ordered to strengthen point at bottom cross roads and make a signallers dugout.

At 8-30 am 2 platoons of the Pioneers wired the forward line, completing it at 1 pm.

At 1 pm the larger portion of the 123 Field Company were sent back to their bivouac - The remainder were sent back at 9 pm, arriving there at 10-15 pm.

At 1 am. rations were brought out to 124 Field Company by their No. 4 section and at 4 am No. 4 and No. 1 sections were sent to relieve Nos. 2 and 3 sections.

Nos. 2 and 3 sections returned to MINDEN at 6 am. while Nos. 1 and 4 sections made strong points at W.S.T. and K. Nos 1 and 4 sections returned at 9 pm. C.R.E. moved his Headquarters to TREUX in the evening.

12th July

123 and 124 Field Companies left WATERLOO JUNCTION at 4 pm and arrived at MEAULTE at 7 pm.

151 Field Company sections arrived at VILLE between 3-30 and 11 am.

The transport of all Companies marched by road under command of O.C. Divisional Train.

C.R.E. with his Headquarters and 151 Field Company (dismounted) left EDGE HILL by ammunition Train at 7-30 pm.

13th July

The train arrived at LONGPRE les TOUS SAINTES at 12-30 am. C.R.E's Headquarters at PONT REMY - 151 Field Company in billets at LONGETTE.

123 and 124 Field Companies arrived at LONGPRE by Motor Bus at 4-30 am and all R.E. (dismounted) left LONGPRE by motor-bus at 8 pm arriving at RUBEMPRE at 11 pm.

C.A. Falcon
Lt. Col.

28-7-16.   C.R.E. 38th Division.

NOTES ON MAMETZ WOOD OBTAINED BY PATROL, 2nd Battn,
ROYAL IRISH REGIMENT, ON NIGHT 3/4TH. JULY.

The wood was entered up to the East and West line passing X.24 central.

The wood is very dense with thick undergrowth in that part which was entered and movement for infantry is not easy. There is a trip wire at the edge of the wood which would not form a serious obstacle by day.

About 100 yards inside the southern face of the wood is a small shallow trench or dip.

There was no prepared work within the area traversed.

STRIP TRENCH is strongly wired and well traversed. Trees from the wood have fallen across the trench and make movement difficult.

WOOD TRENCH is well wired.

Position of machine guns at:----

        S.19.d.7.8   (certain).
        X.24.c.6.4   (suspected).
        X.23.b.5.8   (practically certain).
        ACID DROP COPSE (certain).

The machine guns in ACID DROP COPSE FIRE DIRECTLY DOWN THE valley in S.S.E. direction.

NOTES ON MAMETZ WOOD OBTAINED FROM A FRENCHMAN;
THIS INFORMATION DATES FROM BEFORE THE WAR.

There is a path running from N. to S. at either side of which there are cut willows; the following trees are to be found:-----

1. Oak 9 feet in girth.
2. Birch 2 feet in girth.
3. Beech (only a few of these) 6 feet in girth.
4. And some ash.

The average height of these trees is from 30 to 45 feet. On the N.E. border there is some strong undergrowth of hawthorn and briar. The long narrow strip running down from the wood at the S.W. end is a thicket of tall hornbeam 90 to 120 feet in width.

Confidential (Original)

C R E vol 8

War Diary
of
Headquarters
Royal Engineers
38th Welsh Division
August 1916

Army Form C. 2118

WAR DIARY or INTELLIGENCE SUMMARY

(Erase heading not required.)

Headquarters
Royal Engineer
38th H.Div. Div
August 1916

Place	Date	Hour	Summary of Events and Information	Remarks and references to Appendices
POPERINGHE	1/8/16	10.25 p.	Received 38 Div G.55 of 1/8 instr Coy to take over Second Army.	
G.8.	2/8/16		Received 2nd Army letter 17a Q/8 of 1-8-16. re 123 Field Coy being placed at the disposal of C.E. Second Army.	
Hut 27	3/8/16		123 Field Coy proceed to Second Army. (HR. at Canada Street)	
POPERINGHE	9/8/16		124 Field Coy placed at Disposal of C.E. VIII Corps for work on Elverdinghe Defences. (BHQ Field 23 Belgium.)	
VIII Corps	9/8/16		Two sections of 107 Field Coy placed at disposal of 4th Div. One Section of 107 Field Coy placed at disposal of 29th Div.	
	4/8		124th Field Coy move to Elverdinghe.	
	5/8		Two Sections 107 Field Coy move to YPRES for work under CRE 29 Div. Two Sections 107 Field Coy move to Dugouts on Canal Bank for work under CRE Div.	
	13/8		One Section 123 Field Coy returned to 38th Div for work on rail Bank at BOKSZEELE (See 27).	
	19/8	7.00 a	Received 38 Div Order N.O.63 re release of 4 Div by 38 Div on 21st inst.	

WAR DIARY or INTELLIGENCE SUMMARY

Army Form C. 2118

Headquarters Royal Engineers
58th Welsh Div
August 1916.

Place	Date	Hour	Summary of Events and Information	Remarks and references to Appendices
ESQUELBECQ	21	9.30am	Left Esquelbecq for ST SIXTE CAMP	
ST SIXTE CAMP		10.0am	Relieved 4th Div on front from (Shut 28NW) Skeet St Julien.) C.22.C.75.15 to B.12.d.85.70. (Belgian army on left. 29th Div on Right.)	
58th Div III Corps Area	23rd	12.5	3rd Coy RE R.00 1 Off + 10 OR rejoined Div from Second Army. 1 Off + 10 OR retained for work in ammunition dumps at various rail heads.	See details of Engineer Works as attached

31=8.16

C Allen
Lt Col CRE 58th Div

Details of Work in Hand 21 - 31 Aug. 1916.
Ref. St Julien sheet 28.NW 2. Scale 1/10.000

123rd Fld Coy. Strong Points at :-
Hill Top Farm C.21.d.1.8. Excavating for M.G. emplacements and dug-outs
La Belle Alliance C.21.C.0.7. Excavating and revetting
Wilson Farm C.16.b.5.1. Excavating

1. Officer ½ section attached Second Army for work at Ammunition dumps at various railheads.

174th Field Coy. Strong Points at :-
Sterling Castle J 13 d 44 - Revetting
Skipton Road C.13.b.0.4
Fargate C.7.C.17 - Deepening Communication Trenches & repairs
Work on Fargate Dug-outs C.7.C.17. Excavations and Timbering
Artillery O.P. at C.19.a.9.9
Repairs to Bridges across Ypres Canal
One Section employed on the Elverdinghe Defences working directly under the C.E. VIII Corps.

151st Coy. R.E. Strong Points at -
Turco Farm C.15/C.7.4 - Construction of Concrete M.G. Emplacements & Dug-outs
Highland Farm Defences C.19.b.45: - Preparation of sites for Concrete M.G. Emplacements & Dug-outs
No 17 Butts (Lancashire Farm) C.14.C.73 Revetting & repairing

Pioneers. Repairs to trenches relaying trench boards.
19th Welsh Regt. Revetting & drainage work.

R.E. Vol 9

War Diary
Headquarters
38th Divisional Engineers

September 1916.

WAR DIARY
or
INTELLIGENCE SUMMARY

Army Form C. 2118

PAGE 1

Headquarters
Royal Engineers
58th Welsh Div
Sept 1916

Place	Date	Hour	Summary of Events and Information	Remarks and references to Appendices
SIXTE CAMP Sheet 28 B.L.D III CORPS AREA			Military Situation from C.22.c.75-15.06.B.12.c.83-70 (Refs Sects of Ypres Salient) 29th Div on Right, 3rd Belgian Division Left.	Ref Sheets Sheet 28 NW attached
	8%		1/1 Durham Field Coy R.E. (100/detain) attached to 30th Div for work in back area. Two Sections employed on improvements to camps and construction of horse standings with infantry working parties. One section employed on hut-accumn at WILSON FARM. (C.26.c.45.10).	
	Sept	12.25pm	Received 56th Div Order N°62 re relieve of 2nd Div Troops by this Div by or on 17th inst.	DETAILS OF WORK IN PROGRESS IS ATTACHED
		6.0pm	1/1 Durham Field Coy R.E. to ADSS A to 4th Div.	

Army Form C. 2118

PAGE II

WAR DIARY
or
INTELLIGENCE SUMMARY
(Erase heading not required.)

Headquarters
Royal Engineers
38th Welsh Division
Septr 1916.

Instructions regarding War Diaries and Intelligence Summaries are contained in F. S. Regs., Part II. and the Staff Manual respectively. Title Pages will be prepared in manuscript.

Place	Date	Hour	Summary of Events and Information	Remarks and references to Appendices
TSNTR CAMP.	17th	noon.	Received 38th Div. H.Q. G.S.2. One section of 161 Field Coy R.E. to be placed at the disposal of C.E. VIII Corps for works ELVERDINGHE express. One section under 2nd Lieut PATON attached for this work.	
	22nd		Lt. Col. B. S. Philpotts R.E. arrived & took over duties of C.R.E. - relieved Major L. G. Fulton R.E. One section from each of 123 & 124 & 123 Field Coys return to back billets for work in back area.	

B S Philpotts
Lt Col
C.R.E. 38th Div

SUMMARY OF WORK.
38th Division Engineers.
September.1916.

                      C.21b.5.1

123rd Field Coy,R.E;-   Strong Points; WILSON FARM. C.21.d.1
                HILL TOP.
          Erection of Gum Boot Store.
          Patrol of and Repairs to Canal Bridges.
          Improvement of Canal Defences.
          Patrol of and Repairs to Tramways.
          Repairs to Screening of Ypres-Elverdinghe Rd.
          Erection od Dugouts on Canal Bank.
          General repairs and improvements in
            front line.
          One Section in Back Area from 22nd,
          employed on improvements to Camps, Horse
          Standings, laundries & drying rooms.

                      C.13.a.3.8
                      C.13.b.0.4½.

124th Field Coy.R.E;-   Strong Points; Fargate.
                Skipton Post.
         Erection of Gum Boot store.
         Patrol of and Repairs to Canal Bridges.
         Erection of Dugouts,Fargate & Canal Bank.
         Patrol of and Repairs to Tramways.
         General repairs and improvements in
           front line.
         Repairs to Water trough along Yperlee.
         One Section in Back Area from 22nd,
         employed on improvements to Camps,Horse
         Standings, & drying rooms.

                      C.15.c.2.4
                      C.19.b.4.6

151st Field Coy.R.E;-   Strong Points; Turco Farm.
                Highland Farm   C.27.c.2.6.
                Irish Farm.   C.20.d.0.7.
                La Belle Aliance. C.14.c.2.3
         Completion of Lancashire Dugouts.
         Erection of Screening.
         One Section under VIII Corps at
         Elverdinghe from 17th.

    All Map References for Sheet 28.N.W.

       R-----------

Vol 10

Secret.   Confidential.

Original
War Diary - October - 1916.

Head Quarters, Royal Engineers.
38th (Welsh) Division.

31-10-1916.

WAR DIARY
or
INTELLIGENCE SUMMARY

(Erase heading not required.)

Army Form C. 2118

Headquarters
Royal Engineers
38th (Welsh) Div.
Oct 1916

Place	Date	Hour	Summary of Events and Information	Remarks and references to Appendices
SYSTEM	1916		Holding front line from C.22 c.23.15 to B.22d.95.20 left half Ypres Salient.	
CAMP	3rd		29th Div on Right. 3rd Belgian Div on Left.	
Sheet 28			Use of Tubes made of rabbit netting with gloss wool was found very useful for temporary revetting.	
A.I.d.				
LEFT DIV {4th, 5th, 6th}			55th Div relieved 29th Div on right section of Ypres Salient.	
VIII Corps	9th		Asst. DR proceed on leave to England. 2 Lieut Paton arriving camp Aga.	
AREA	16th, 17th		Heavy rain.	
	18th		Owing to heavy rain Yperlee flooded causing damage to Aqueduct, also rose above level of Aqueduct & polluted water supply. Immediate steps were taken to adjust matters.	

WAR DIARY or INTELLIGENCE SUMMARY

Army Form C. 2118

Page II

Headquarters Royal Engineers
38th Welsh Division

October 1916.

Place	Date	Hour	Summary of Events and Information	Remarks and references to Appendices
SISNIE CAMP	10th		AAjt returned from leave.	For summary of work on same see the attached.
	23rd		Purchased 37000 bricks at Bailleul for work on horse standings in Kivernel. Bricks allotted to 38 Divn, 33rd Divn & VIII Corps Heavy Arty to be by us rway.	
	28th		Dining Room in Reperoy Hut completed & put in use.	
	30th		Water supply for horse troughs at 113 Bde Transport Lines (Pont b.) completed	

EYP Lewis Lt. Col.
CRE 38 Div

Vol. XI

Secret

Original

War Diary

November 1916

Headquarters, Royal Engineers

38th Division

WAR DIARY or INTELLIGENCE SUMMARY

Army Form

Headquarters Royal Engineers
58th Welsh Div.
November 1916

(Erase heading not required.)

Instructions regarding War Diaries and Intelligence Summaries are contained in F.S. Regs., Part II. and the Staff Manual respectively. Title Pages will be prepared in manuscript.

Place	Date	Hour	Summary of Events and Information	Remarks and references to Appendices
SIXTK	Nov		Holding front line from C22C.75.15 to B12.d.35.70 (Incl.) (Right to Left) (Relief to be arranged). 53rd Div on Right & Belgian Div on Left.	Summary of trench work in progress as entered on attached.
CAMP				
R.1.d				
Regt.Hd				
VIII Corps	16th		Usual 3 days class for Officers NCO & of Corps R.E. between 14th to 16th Nov. Lectures, Trench Repairs, Drainage, Revetting, use of explosives. Class conducted by the Instructional Sub.	
Diss	17th		Raid on enemy trenches at ... by 4th East Lancs Reg (200 men) accompanied by Sapper (3 N.C.O + 9 men). Sappers ento Cogeux demolition work. (see attached report).	

1875 Wt. W593/826 1,000,000 4/15 J.B.C. & A. A.D.S.S./Forms/C.2118.

WAR DIARY or INTELLIGENCE SUMMARY

Army Form C. 2118

Page 11

Headquarters Royal Engineers 39th Divl. Div.

Nov 1916.

Place	Date	Hour	Summary of Events and Information	Remarks and references to Appendices
	19th		Arrival of 39th Dn in Corps reserve area.	
	24th		Received Orders No 9 to relief of French 79 (West) 50th Territorial Regt at 2nd Belgian Div. by 118 Bde of 39th Div the taking over of RE work in that sector by the 2 3 x Field Coys 39 Div. on 25th Novr.	
	26.		Received 39th Div Order No. 41 re relief of French 79th Territorial Reg. in the Boesinghe sector, by the 118 Bde. Relief was to be all complete by 8 p.m. on Nov 30th. Corps Boundary extended to VIIICorps B5 a 7.1, Bn a 7.7, B11 a 2.8.6; Chapelle (inclusive) Boyau de Boesinghe at B7 d 5.8.0. B9 a 2.85, B10 b 1.8½, B10 c 3.4, B7 c 6.0. B7 c 0.9. B7 c 0.7½, A12 c 3.2. A8 d 3.8½ thence east [?] tower [?]	

WAR DIARY
or
INTELLIGENCE SUMMARY

Army Form C. 2118

Place	Date	Hour	Summary of Events and Information	Remarks and references to Appendices
	24th		2nd Class fit. Officers & N.C.Os of Reserve Bde commenced (Holly) Class conducted by 2nd Lt Carroll 103 Field Coy R.E.	
	28th		23rd Field Coy R.E. arrived at F. corp. A.16.C. end.	
	29th		Commenced enlarging to Divisional Laundry at Potenyse to accomodate extra work also 1 to attach nursery for Sui . work undertaken by 1 section of 23rd Field Coy R.E.	
	30th	11.00am	Received phone message from 38th Div. G.a. 1 sect of Sigs detailed for work in Rifle Ranges nr. TYR Q.023 N.W. ST.O.N.F.R. 157 Field Coy attd CRE Orders No.12 issued	

Wm Rushworth
Lt Col
C.R.E. 38th Div.

SUMMARY OF WORK
38th Divisional Engineers
NOVEMBER.1916
****

123rd Field Coy R.E.

Wilson Farm. Strong Point. C.21.b.4.1 ;- Draining,excavating and
           revetting continued. Box drains completed.
Signallers Dugouts,C.d.0.4½.4;- Concrete completed.
Front Line. Reclaiming of Atlas Trench and Yorks and Lancs trench
           continued, draining,revetting and sandbagging.
Gum Boot store. C.25.c.9.2.;-   Completed.
Tramways.   Patrolled and repairs. Extension to front line completed.
Bridges.   Bridges patrolled and necessary repairs executed.
Yperlee Water trough;-   Repaired where necessary.
Road Bridge, C.d.4½.3½.;-   Erected.
Fargate H.T.M.Emplacement, C.13.d.0.9,;- Commenced.
Gunpits, C.25.d.6.1,;-   Commencedz
Back Area. Water Supply, E.Camp. G.4.b.5.2.
           Improvements 113 Bde Transport Lines, A,14.b.7.8.
           Water Supply, D.Camp,A,28.d.7.7.
           Horse Standings,115 M.G.Coy, S.Camp, A.23.c.1.5.
           Erection of cookhouses, N.Camp. 10th Welsh,Sh.27. F.27a57.
           Improvements to Officers Mess, P.Camp.A,28.d.4.8.

124th Field Coy, R.E.

Bridges.   Patrolled and repaired.
Gumboot Store. Completed.
Signallers Dugouts; Concreting completed.
Tramways.   Several portions completed, others relaid and repaired.
Skipton Post.   Strong Point, C,13.b.0.4½.   Revetting new trenches
           and concreting continued.
Fargate,   Strong Point, C,13.c.3.8. and Fargate Dugouts; Concreting
           sandbagging and revetting continued, also drainage.
Front Line; E.23. E.26. E.27, and White Trench,C.13.8; Repairing and
           draining and revetting, fixing new dugouts.
Fusilier Drain ; and Inkerman; Drainage continued.
Back Area. Erection of new Horse Standings, A,15.b.5.9.
           Repairs to Curragh Hut, D.Camp, A,28.d.7.7.
           New drying room, Courthove.
           Improvements, Divisional School.

151st Field Coy, R.E.

Strong Points; Concreting and drainage @ revetting work continued;
           Turco Farm, C,15.c.2.4.
           Highland Farm, C,19.b.4.6
           Irish Farm, C,27.c.2.6. Signallers dugout completed.
           Hill Top,C,21.d.1.
           La Belle Aliance,C.20.d.0.7, new communication trenches.
Lancashire Dugouts; C.14.c.2.3, M,G,Empl. trenches, @ dugouts in
           course of erection.
Tramways,   Repaired and relaid, new track laid.

Report on Raid held on Nov 17th

Three N.C.O's and nine Sappers of the 123rd Field Company.R.E., took part in the Raid on High Command Redoubt last night, the 17th instant. They were all employed on Demolition work. I have questioned each N.C.O and man, and from the information they have given me I beg to report as follows:-

The Sappers entered in 2 parties. The Right Party of 2 N.C.O's and 5 Sappers under the command of Sergeant R.P.Sheppard followed immediately behind Z Part of the Raiders. The Left Party of 1 N.C.O and 4 Sappers under Corporal W.R.Ferris followed behind X Party.
Sergt.Sheppard's Party came across a Machine Gun Emplacement in what was generally supposed to be the Support Line; it had recently been built, and the centreing was still in position. A charge of 16 lbs of Guncotton was placed in the loophole and tamped. A Sketch of this M.G.E is attached marked 'A'.

About 10 yards away they found an O.P – Sketch attached marked 'B'. Sergt Sheppard entered this O.P followed by his men. They found seven Germans, one being a Sergt.Major. These were taken prisoners, and were handed over to an Infantry Party, who took them back to our Lines. Two charges each of 16.lbs of Guncotton were placed here. There were 8 armoured cables leading into the Dugout. The Sappers found a quantity of papers and maps, also a periscope, which was unscrewed from the wall. These articles were handed over to the Infantry.

Corporal Ferris' Party proceeded to the Left with instructions to make a breach in the parapet, and also to demolish anything else of importance. One charge of 32 lbs. of Guncotton was placed in a hole in the highest part of the parapet. Section attached marked 'C'. An observation Cupola was found a short distance away, and a charge placed against it. Sketch of Cupola is attached marked 'D'.

A Concrete Dugout about 8.ft square inside, 4 yards away had been demolished by a Shell. After placing the charges Corporal Ferris and his men made a search in the immediate vicinity and found a Machine Gun in an Open Emplacement on the parapet. They took it out, and as they had instructions to hand everything over to the Infantry they called the nearest man and told him to take it back. At this time a German rose up from the Ground, where he had been lying, and advanced on Corporal Ferris, who knocked him out with his knobkerry.

Instructions had been given that the fuses had to be lit on the sounding of the third Whistle, when all the Infantry men would be clear of the German Trenches. All charges were successfully exploded, and considering the sizes of the works and the quantity of the explosive used I feel certain that the demolitions were successful.

All the R.E. returned safely to our Lines, but one man, Sapper J.Barnett, was wounded by a Shell on the Trench Grids between D.20 and Turco Farm.

                        sd.   I.W.Lamonby.
                                          Major. R.E
18.11.16.   O.C.123rd Field Coy. R.E

A

REINFORCED CONCRETE
M.G
EMPLACEMENT.

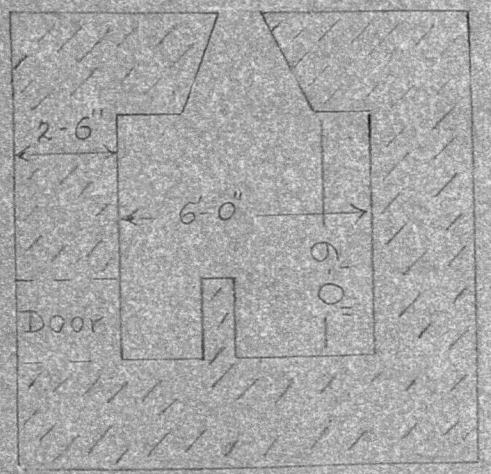

Height inside 4ft.
Roof 3ft. thick.

B

REINFORCED CONCRETE DUGOUT
AND O.P

Periscope.

Observation Post 3ft by
8ft by 8ft high.

Tunnelled passage 2'6" x8ft.

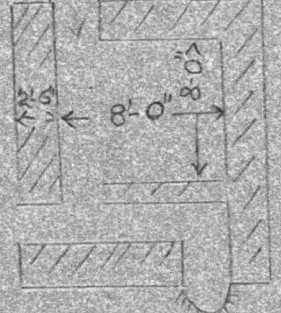

Excavation in Progress.

Height inside 5ft.
Roff total thickness 4ft.

C

SECTION OF GERMAN PARAPET.

Revetted with brushwood hurdles and pickets.

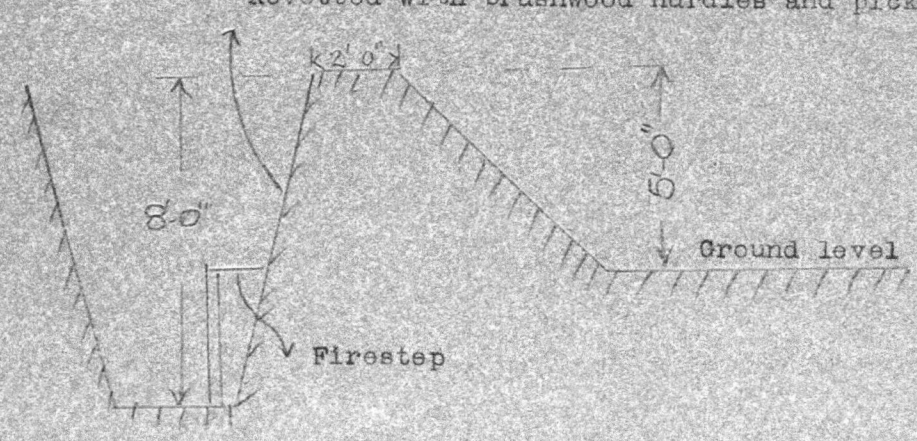

Firestep

Ground level

D

CONCRETE O.P.

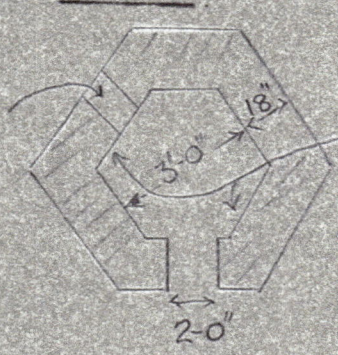

Loophole 4in square.

Lined with ¼in. plate steel

3'0"   18"   2'0"

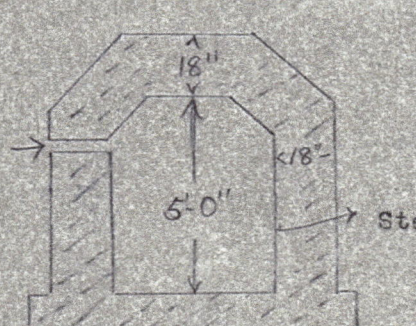

Loophole 4in square

18"   18"   5'0"

Steel Plates

Vol 12

Secret   Original

— War Diary —
Headquarters Royal Engineers
— 38th Division —

— December 1916 —

31.12.16

WAR DIARY
or
INTELLIGENCE SUMMARY

Army Form C. 2118

Headquarters
Royal Engineers
38th Division

December 1916

Place	Date	Hour	Summary of Events and Information	Remarks and references to Appendices
ST SIXTE	DEC		Holding Front Line from C22 C. 75.15 to B6 C 2.5 (Right Sector Ypres Salient)	
CAMP.			2nd Division of Right. Belgian Queen on left.	
Shew 22	1st		107 Field Coy RE relieved by 225 Field Coy RE.	
A.I.D.			107 Field Coy RE proceed to HOOKE N'STOMER to entrain with transport under CRE 39th Div. for Second Army.	
Left Hd.			Confirmation of relief of June of 79th Territorial Reg by 113th Bn.	
VIII Corps			234 Field Coy RE take over new RE work in new sector.	
Area.	7th		Received preliminary orders (38a/n°65253) re relief of 38th Div by 39th Div.	
	9th		Received 38th Div O.O.72. Issue CRE orders 70H	
	11th		123 Field Coy RE to Hill Top Sector relieved 23rd Field Coy RE in Bourght Sector	
			234 Field Coy RE to Bourght Sector relieved 123 Field Coy RE Hill Top Sector	
	13th		227 Field Coy RE relieved 124 Field Coy RE in Lancashire Bombers	
	14th		124 Field Coy RE move to billets at MERCKEGHEM (A27 a c4.c. 27)	
		11.00	CRE 38 Div relieved by CRE 39 Div. REHQ move from ST SIXTE Camp to ESQUELDECQ (C8 c4c.c.27)	

WAR DIARY
or
INTELLIGENCE SUMMARY

(Erase heading not required.)

Army Form C. 2118

Headquarters Royal Engineers
36 Welsh Division
December 1916

Place	Date	Hour	Summary of Events and Information	Remarks and references to Appendices
EQUELBECQ	25		124 Field Coy RE went to billets in WATTEN (Sg C3 Sheet Hazebrouck 5A) for bridging training on the Canal de la COLME.	
["Keer 2"]				
	30th		124 Field Coy RE relieved 123 Field Coy RE in the Busseboom Sector. 123 Field Coy RE proceed to WATTEN for bridging training.	[signature] Lt Col RE CRE 36th Div

Summary of Work.
38th Division Engineers.
October 1916.

123 Field Coy. R.E.

Strong Point. Wilson Farm. C.21.b.5.1. Repairing, draining and excavation continued.	
Canal Bridges.	Patrolled and repaired.
Tramways.	Patrolled and repaired. New siding near Essex Farm completed. Other passing sidings in course of construction.
Water troughs along Yperlee.	Repaired where necessary.
Dugouts.	Brigade dugouts erected and Signallers dugout in course of construction. General improvements
Gum boot store.	Extension of existing shed completed.
Water supply.	6 tanks and 2 water boxes erected.
Front Line.	Repairing, draining, hurdling trenches. re-laying grids. Re-making Yorkshire and Lancashire Trench. Drain from Atlas Trench to Willows.
Back area work.	Drying room Poperinghe. Water supplies for 113 Brigade Transport Lines, 11 S.W.B. 17 R.W.F E Camp. Work in horse lines 16th Welsh and 115 Machine Gun Co.
Levelling.	Sections taken in Front Line.

124 Field Coy. R.E.

Bridges.	Patrolled and repaired. Screens erected.
Tramways.	Patrolled and repaired. 200 yards extension to approach to Colne Valley.
Dugouts.	Dugouts erected. Signallers. Concreting etc.
Gun Boot Store.	Work continued.
Strong points.	Skipton Post. C.13.b.0.4½. Fargate. C.13.a.3.8.
Fargate dugout.	Excavation and concreting.
Artillery O.P.	Floor of dugout made water tight.
Water supply.	Tanks and troughing erected.
Yperlee Bank.	Track completed and Bank repairs.
Gauges.	Water level gauges fixed at (1) Bridge 6W. centre of Canal. (2) Yperlee stream opp. Coy. Hd.Qrs. and daily readings taken.
Kitchens.	Work on Brigade and Company kitchens.
Levelling.	Levelling of trenches completed for whole of front line where possible.
Miscellaneous.	Laying and wiring new duckboard track.
Front Line.	White Trench. 75' of new trench. Work on front trenches. Front line C.13.2. C.14.6. C.13.3. C.14.7. C.13.4. C.14.8. C.13.8. C.14.9.
Back area work.	Commencement of erection of Drying room at Couthove Laundry and work on filter tanks. Improvements to roads and drains in P. Camp Work on horse standings at A.16.a.1.0.

(1)

151 Field Coy. R.E.

    Strong points.   Turco Farm. C.15.c.2.4.
                                 ~~Highland Farm. C.16.b.4.6.~~
                                  Lancashire Dugouts. C.14.c.2.3.
                                  Irish Farm. C.27.a.2.6.
                                  Hilltop. C.21.d.1.
                                  La Belle Alliance. C.20.d.0.7.

    Screening.

    Back area work.   Defences at Elverdinghe.

Secret. Original

WO R9 38 P
Vol 3

War Diary
Headquarters
Royal Engineers
38th Welsh Div.
January 1917

WAR DIARY or **INTELLIGENCE SUMMARY**
(Erase heading not required.)

Army Form C. 2118

Headquarters Royal Engineers 38th Welsh Div
January 1917

Page 1

Place	Date	Hour	Summary of Events and Information	Remarks and references to Appendices
PROVEN BECQ	1st			
Sheet 27	8th		Received 38th Div Order re relief of 39th Div by 38th Div in the left sector VIII Corps front between 12 & 15th	
III Corps				
Proven	12th		123 Field Coy RE moves from Watou by tram to Poperinghe & relieves the 234th Field Coy RE in the Hill Top Sector.	
Div Area			151 Field Coy RE moves from Houtke to Poperinghe by tram and relieves 12th Field Coy RE in Boesinghe Sector.	
	13		124 Field Coy RE relieves 227 Field Coy RE in Lancashire Farm Sector	
	14		2/1 Welsh Field Coy (53 Div) relieves 225 Field Coy RE in work Shotwork Hilltop & Lancashire Farm Sector	

WAR DIARY or INTELLIGENCE SUMMARY

Army Form C. 2118

H.Q. Royal Engineers 39 Div

January 1917

Page 11

Place	Date	Hour	Summary of Events and Information	Remarks and references to Appendices
SIXTK ... DIV ... FT DIV ... Corps ...	15		RE Headquarters moved from EQUELBECQ to SYS XTE Camp. CRE 8th Div Relieves CRE 39 Div.	
			39th Div on Right. 3rd Belgian Div on Left.	
	24		1/1 W. & W. Lanc Field Coy Relieves 2/1 W. Lanc Fd Coy R.E.	
	26		Outbreak of fire at R.E. Headquarters. All office secret documents, papers, maps destroyed, including important A/c & Cash book.	

W.W. Dies Lt Col
CRE 39 DIV

Secret

Vol 14

Original

War Diary

Headquarters Royal Engineers
38" Division

February 1917

Page 1   Army Form C. 2118

WAR DIARY
or
INTELLIGENCE SUMMARY
(Erase heading not required.)

Headquarters Royal Engineers 28th Welsh Division

February 1917

Place	Date	Hour	Summary of Events and Information	Remarks and references to Appendices
ST SIXTE R.I.d Sheet 28	1st		39 Div in Rafts 6th Belgian Div in Left (Cid) Severe frost continues. Excavating work in progress. Workshops pipes filled with Ammonal were driven frozen crust on exploded with success. Volley stones. Shortage of fillows, R.E Stores. Saw Frost in Roof Cons. Shingle + sand	
Left Div VIII Corps Area	2nd 27th			
	9th 10 to 14		Shortage of fillows, R.E.Stores. Timber. Cl Huts, Roofing. Saw Shingle + sand. Relief of 6th Belgian Div in Left by 6th Belgian Div.	
	16th		Has precaution in force for 6 days. Shortage of fillows, R.E.Stores. Felt. Shingle Sand. Timber [illegible].	
	18th		Relief of 39th Div in Rafts by 55th Div. 419 Fer Co, (55 Div) attached 38 Div received by 227 FC Co (39 Div)	
	26th		2/2 F.Sd. Coy R.E reported 39th Div	

Page ii

WAR DIARY
or
INTELLIGENCE SUMMARY
(Erase heading not required.)

Army Form C. 2118

Headquarters Royal Engineers 38th Welsh Div February 1917

Instructions regarding War Diaries and Intelligence Summaries are contained in F. S. Regs, Part II. and the Staff Manual respectively. Title Pages will be prepared in manuscript.

Place	Date	Hour	Summary of Events and Information	Remarks and references to Appendices
SISXTK H.I.A. Sheet 28 Lafer Ord VIII Corps Area	23		55th Div on Right 6th Belgian Div on Left. Shortage of following R.E. Stores: Roof Iron, Pickets, Sand Bags, Kegs (elegumfrances).	
	24th		Normal Traffic crossing river after has Precautions.	
	27/28		Readjustment of Div Boundary. Front line taken over by 55th Div from C.22.c.7.1. to C.21.b.6.4. New Boundary C.21.b.6.4. C.21.a.2.4. Bridge 2a (C.25.a.2.2.) inclusive.	Ref Syst 29/11/17

[signature] Lt. Col. C.R.E. 58 Div.

Confidential　　　　　　　　　　Original

War Diary.

Headquarters.
Royal Engineers
38th Div.

March 1917

Confidential　　　　　　　　　　Original

WAR DIARY
or
INTELLIGENCE SUMMARY

Army Form C. 2118

Headquarters Coy Engineers 38th Welsh Div.
March 1917

Page 1

Place	Date	Hour	Summary of Events and Information	Remarks and references to Appendices
STS/XTE A,b, Shut 28	2nd		55th Divn on Right. 6th Belgian Div on Left. Shortage of sawn timber and sand, slight improvement in other concreting material.	
Left Divn VIII Corps Area	5th		Ypres – Boesinghe Branch line damaged by shellfire. Delivery of RE stores by rail not interrupted.	
	9th		Shortage of shingle sand and sawn timber, slight improvement in corrugated iron sheeting and Roofing Felt.	

WAR DIARY or INTELLIGENCE SUMMARY

Army Form C. 2118

Page 11

Headquarters Royal Engineers 58th (Welsh?) Division
March 1917

Place	Date	Hour	Summary of Events and Information	Remarks and references to Appendices
	16th		Shortage of Roadmetal, Sawn Timber, Loop-hole and Screw Pickets, Screw Pickets.	
	22nd		Received instruction from O.C. VIII Corps re: carry of Timber. None to be used for other than front line work without authority.	
	23rd		Shortage of Sawn Roadmetal — O.C. Sawn Timber. Dependent solely on trees sewn at Div. R.E. Park for supply of Timber.	
	30th		Scarcity of all Timber. Shortage of Sand Ship, &c., Roadmetal & Shells.	

OHSMsWatts
Lt. Col.
C.R.E. 58th Div.

WAR DIARY
or
INTELLIGENCE SUMMARY.

Army Form C. 2118.

(Erase heading not required.)

Part 9

Hour, Date, Place	Summary of Events and Information	Remarks and references to Appendices
Sept. 19th SUZANNE.	Nothing to record except that 2 Coys and details 15/R Warwick Regt completed platoon period of training at 5pm in A.3. and A.4. and started company period.	
Sept. 20th SUZANNE.	Situation normal. Several active wire parties and Lewis guns during night 19/20 Sept. During evening 1/Edwards relieved 1/Seconds in A.4. and 1/Seconds moved to billets in SUZANNE. 1/Manchesters relieved 1/DCLI in A.2. and 1/DCLI took over billets in SUZANNE. 1/Manchesters relieved 1/Warwickings where 1/Manchesters took over MARICOURT defences.	
Sept. 21st SUZANNE.	Quiet night and day. Two Coys 15/R Warwicks completed 3rd period of training on Coys and withdraw to huts at SUZANNE.	
Sept. 22nd SUZANNE.	Quiet night but enemy's artillery active during day. 1/Manchesters took over A.2 from 1/DCLI who withdrew to billets in SUZANNE. 1/Manchesters took over A.3. from 1/Warwickings who took over MARICOURT defences. 15/R Warwicks took over A.4. from 1/Edwards who withdrew to billets vacated by 1/Edwards in SUZANNE.	
Sept. 23rd SUZANNE.	Quiet night but unusual activity on part of enemy artillery throughout front of Sector during day.	

WAR DIARY or INTELLIGENCE SUMMARY

Army Form C. 2118

Headquarters Royal Engineers 58th (2/1st) Wilts Division
April 1917

Page 1

(Erase heading not required.)

Place	Date	Hour	Summary of Events and Information	Remarks and references to Appendices
TSIXTK			58th Div on Right. 6" Belgian Div on Left.	
R.E.	6th		R.E. Stores. Continued shortage of sawn timber	
Hdqrs 2/8				
Left Div				
VIII Corps				
Amin	15th		R.E. Stores. Continued shortage of sawn timber. Supply of Komp & and "A" frame improved.	
	16th		Received 3rd R.E. Order 1787 re laying one of Right Div Area to 39th R Div on night 17/18.	
	17th		39th Div took over front line from C.14 c 2.6½ to C.21 c 8.9. One work out of line C.14 d 2 5.6½. C 20 c 5 6. Pom Cottage budget handed over to 39th Div.	
	20th		R.E. Stores Shortage of sawn timber	

WAR DIARY or INTELLIGENCE SUMMARY

Army Form C. 2118

Headquarters R.E. 58th Welsh Division
April 1917

Page 11

Place	Date	Hour	Summary of Events and Information	Remarks and references to Appendices
	21st		R.E. Stores. Shortage of Lawn Tubes. Steel Shelters & Cement.	
	Night 29-30		Demolition party of 1 NCO & 4 Sappers accompanied Raiding Party in Raid on Enemy Trenches. Two Gallon Petrol tins filled with Ammonal were used as mobile charges. One Dugout, one Emplacement, one concrete work in course of erection destroyed.	

J.W. Puleston Lt. Col.
CRE 58th Div.

Army Form C. 2118.

WAR DIARY
INTELLIGENCE SUMMARY
(Erase heading not required.)

Instructions regarding War Diaries and Intelligence Summaries are contained in F.S. Regs., Part II. and the Staff Manual respectively. Title pages will be prepared in manuscript.

PMD 9

Hour, Date, Place	Summary of Events and Information	Remarks and references to Appendices
Dect. 19th SUZANNE.	Nothing to record except that 2 Coys and details 15/R Hamuck Regt completed shortened period of training at 5pm in A.3 and A.4 and started company period.	
Dect. 20th SUZANNE.	Situation normal. Several rumours active with snipers and Lewis guns during night 19/20 Dect. During evening 1/Edmunds relieved 1/Devons in A.4 and 1/Devons moved to billets in SUZANNE. 17/Manchesters relieved 1/DCLI in A.2 and 1/DCLI took over billets in SUZANNE. 7/Manchesters relieved 7/manchesters in A.3 and 7/manchesters took over MARICOURT defences.	
Dect. 21st SUZANNE.	Quiet night and day. Two Coys 1/R Hamucks completed 3rd period of training in Coys and withdrew to tents at SUZANNE.	
Dect. 22nd SUZANNE.	Quiet night but enemy's artillery active during day. 17/Manchesters took over A.2 from 1/DCLI who withdrew to billets in SUZANNE. 7/Manchesters took over A.3 from 7/Manchesters in SUZANNE who took over MARICOURT defence. 15/R Hamucks took over A.4 from 1/Edmunds who withdrew to billets vacated by Edmunds in SUZANNE.	
Dect. 23rd SUZANNE.	Quiet night but unusual activity on part of enemy artillery throughout front of sector during day	

WAR DIARY *or* **INTELLIGENCE SUMMARY**

Army Form C. 2118

Headquarters Royal Engineers 35th (Ulster) Division
Page 1
May 1917

Place	Date	Hour	Summary of Events and Information	Remarks and references to Appendices
O.S.K.T.E.	Night 30 April / 1 May		35th Division on right. H. Belgian Div on left. Revd on enemy's trenches accompanied by party of 1760 - 13 Sappers for demolition purposes. 5 Concrete dugouts & Concrete M.G. Emplacement & Heavy Timbered dugouts were destroyed. Burs stollen Pelet. This filled with ammunal wine used as charges.	
A.D.			Supply of R.E. Stores	
Hill 28	4th		Shortage of - General	
Hope Dry				
VIII Corps				
Open				
	15th		Supply of R.E. Stores Continued shortage of Duckboards & Cement.	

WAR DIARY or INTELLIGENCE SUMMARY

Army Form C. 2118

Place	Date	Hour	Summary of Events and Information	Remarks and references to Appendices
	19th		151 Field Coy RE handed over work in BOESINGHE sector to D. Coy 19th Welsh Miners and proceeded to WATTEN (N.ST.OMER) for training purposes.	
	18th		Supply of R.E. Stores continued. Shortage of ___ & Cement.	
	22nd		No 6 Army Tramways Coy arrived to take over Tramways in the area.	
	23rd		288th Army Troops Coy RE arrived for work near CRE 30 Div. Commenced work on forward roads.	
	25th		Supply of RE Stores continued. Shortage of ___ & Cement.	
	28th		217 Army Troops Coy RE arrived for work in the area.	
	28th		151 Field Coy RE returned from Watten & relieved 123 Field Coy RE in the Lancashire Farm Sector on the night 28th 29th.	
	29th		123 Field Coy RE proceeded to Watten for training purposes.	

D.S.Plimmer Lt.Col
CRE 38 Div.

Secret.

Original
War Diary.
Headquarters Royal Engineers
38th Division

June 1917

Army Form C. 2118

WAR DIARY
or
INTELLIGENCE SUMMARY

(Erase heading not required.)

Headquarters RE
39th Field Division
June 1917

Instructions regarding War Diaries and Intelligence Summaries are contained in F.S. Regs., Part II. and the Staff Manual respectively. Title Pages will be prepared in manuscript. Page 1

Place	Date	Hour	Summary of Events and Information	Remarks and references to Appendices
SXATE			39th Div gf Right 4th Division Div on Left	
CAMP				
V / a.				
ccep 28	10th		R.E.H.Q. moved from St SIXTE CAMP to Camp at R.E.C.S.S.	
A.D.X	10th	5.0 pm	Fifth Army took over VIII Corps Front.	
VIII Corps			Stock of 5" shells (50,000) at RE Park Poachlock taken by 5th Army as Army Reserve.	
	11th		XIV Corps took over 38th Divl Front.	
			(27 ATCoy)	
	15th		XVIII Corps took over Poserlor to RE Park. Temporary Divl RE Dump formed at A16 a 2.2 in Wood. 123 Field Coy RK relieved from training and relieved 12th Field Coy RE in the Island of Siebot	

Army Form C. 2118

WAR DIARY
or
INTELLIGENCE SUMMARY
(Erase heading not required.)

Instructions regarding War Diaries and Intelligence Summaries are contained in F. S. Regs., Part II. *page 11* and the Staff Manual respectively. Title Pages will be prepared in manuscript.

Place	Date	Hour	Summary of Events and Information	Remarks and references to Appendices
	14th		132nd Field Coy R.E. proceed to Watten for training.	
	16th		Handed over to H.Qrs. Guthrie Farm C.11 a 2.6. to C.11 a 4.-0. New Boundary C.11 a 4.-0, C.13 a 7½ 5. C.19 a 5.8. C.19 a 5.2	
	18th		XVIII Corps refuse to share about 10 truckloads of "intake cuts" left at Paillock R.E. Park (n) 38 D1. Application to XIV Corps without result.	
	19th		Guards Division take over Borough Sector. Left Divl Boundary now B12 a 8.4. - B12 a 12.5. B18 a 0.6. - B16 b.o.5.	
	23		132 Field Coy R.E. move from Watten to ROMBLY arriving there 24th.	

1875 Wt. W593/826 1,000,000 4/17 J.B.C.&A. A.D.S.S./Forms/C. 2118.

WAR DIARY
or
INTELLIGENCE SUMMARY

Army Form C. 2118

Page III

Place	Date	Hour	Summary of Events and Information	Remarks and references to Appendices
	27th		124th Field Coy RE moved from ROMBLY to BOIS COURT. New Divisional RE Park started at the XIV Corps RE Park at ONDANK A.S.C. Camp (Sheet 28).	
	28/29		151 Field Coy RE relieved by 447 Field Coy RE in the Zwaanhof Sector.	
	29th		151 Field Coy proceed to HERZEELE for work under CE XIV Corps on tanks bridges. RE HQ moves from CRE 38 Div relieved by CRE 29 Div. HQ 38 Div move from Dragon Camp A16.B. to TORRENT POSTS	

J.B. Plunkett Lt Col
CRE 38 Div.

Vol 18 Secret

Original War Diary

Headquarters
 Royal Engineers
  38th Division

July 1917

1-8-1917

Army Form C. 2118.

WAR DIARY
or
INTELLIGENCE SUMMARY
(Erase heading not required.)

Page 1 Headquarters
Royal Engineers
38 Division
July 1917

Hour, Date, Place	Summary of Events and Information	Remarks and references to Appendices
MORBECQUE FORTS. 1st July 1917	The 38th Division (less Artillery, 123 Fd and 151st Field Co R.E. and 19th (Pioneer) Bttn Welsh Regiment) in St Hilaire, area for Divisional training. Infantry Brigades and 124 Field Co R.E. employed making the replica of trenches in the 2 WAANOF Sector. Farm implements (ploughs etc) hired locally for cutting crops and marking out trenches for tramways, Railway, etc.	
2nd	Continued work as for 1st.	
3rd	Capt G.V. Morgan R.E. reported from 124 Field Co R.E. reported for duty as Adjutant. Lieut C.H. Brazel adjutant R.E. proceeded to 124 Field Co R.E. for duty as Recconn-in-Command.	
4th	Application made to Army advanced R.E. Park. Letter for full size and miniature targets for use on training ground. Full size targets could not be supplied. Timber, Canvas and paper obtained by special authority from	

WAR DIARY
or
INTELLIGENCE SUMMARY.
(Erase heading not required.)

Army Form C. 2118.

Page 4

Hour, Date, Place	Summary of Events and Information	Remarks and references to Appendices
Nonancourt	Cmd. 4th Chief Engineer 1st Army, for musing 500 file in target, and 124 fire C.Rts instructed to make them.	
July		
5th	Work continued in training area, competitors replies training for fire firing.	
6th	do for 5th	
7th	do	
8th	do	
9th	do	
10th	do	
11th	do Plans prepared for Strong Point of Cruciform pattern.	
12th	Attack carried out as laid down in Divl training operation orders over the replica of trenches, south and west of Enguinegatte, in the St Hilaire training area.	
13th	Trenches in the training area filled in and ground cleared up generally.	
14th	Plans prepared for Strong Point other than cruciform pattern.	

Army Form C. 2118.

WAR DIARY
or
INTELLIGENCE SUMMARY.
(Erase heading not required.)

Page III

Hour, Date, Place	Summary of Events and Information	Remarks and references to Appendices
Movement fords St Hilaire Training area	July 1917	
	15th All surplus R.E. material for training returned to No 4 R.E. Park (1st Army).	
	16th 124 Field C.R.E. proceeded from St Hilaire training area. By route march to the Steenbecque area.	
	17th 124 Field C.R.E. proceeded from Steenbecque area to Caestre area.	
	18th " " " " Caestre area to Eecke area	
	19th " " " " Eecke area to Proven area.	
	" 38th Div H.Q. moved from Mount Jordis (St Hilaire Training Area to Proven. Colincamps Rd) by CRE with Field Co Commanders. Preparing to take over	
Proven Shed 27	20th H.Q. at Camp at Proven.	
F.Y. Central	The Zwaanhof Sector, Ypres Salient.	
	21st 124 Field Co R.E. relieved the Kent Field C.R.E. (29th Div)	15th ? wounded one OR
	in the Zwaanhof sector Ypres Salient. 124 ? Co R.E. Rd killed during relief.	
	38th Division Headquarters relieved 29th Division Headquarters and moved to Brazos Camp.	
	G.O.C. 38 Division assumed Command of the Zwaanhof sector at 10 a.m.	

WAR DIARY
or
INTELLIGENCE SUMMARY.
(Erase heading not required.)

Army Form C. 2118.

Page IV

Instructions regarding War Diaries and Intelligence Summaries are contained in F.S. Regs., Part II. and the Staff Manual respectively. Title pages will be prepared in manuscript.

Hour, Date, Place	Summary of Events and Information	Remarks and references to Appendices
Dragon Camp. July 1917 Map ref. Sheet 28	21st 131st Field Co. R.E. relieved 133 Field Co R.E. in the 2nd army of Sector. 133 Field Co. R.E. proceeded to S. Camp.	
	22nd Not. Enemy H.V. Gun active on back areas. 5 Light Railway Trucks loaded up at R.E. Park and despatched forward on Light Railway. These were smashed in succession and train failed to get to destination. Heavy Artillery duels in the afternoon. Relief continued. Train and forward again to forward Dumps with R.E. material. Failed to get through due to line smashed by shell fire.	
	23rd Artillery activity continuing, back areas shelled.	
	24th H.V. Gun during the night. Efforts again made to send R.E. material forward on Light Railway, successful for the first time. Artillery activity continuous. Canal Bank and Trenches Ready. shell with Gas shells. Casualties in 124 J.O.C.R.E. Major D. Baird R.E. Officer Commanding and 32 O.R. Gassed and evacuated to Hospital. Efforts again made to send R.E. material forward on Light Railway, failed + got through.	
	25th Artillery activity increased and enemy shelled Canal Bank and Trenches. and back areas very heavily. Efforts again made to send R.E. material forward to R.E. Dumps. Train failed to get through. Desired not to use the Light Railway again.	
	26th Heavy bombardment continues. Major J. McMurtrie R.E. O.C. 131 Field Co. R.E. Killed in Target Camp zoned by enemy shell fire.	
	27th Heavy bombardment continues. Reports received from the Major Corps T.O.J. no enemy to be seen in the enemy Trenches near Steenbeck. Reserve orders from Div H.Q. for all	

Army Form C. 2118.

WAR DIARY
or
INTELLIGENCE SUMMARY.
(Erase heading not required.)

Page V

Instructions regarding War Diaries and Intelligence Summaries are contained in F. S. Regs., Part II. and the Staff Manual respectively. Title pages will be prepared in manuscript.

Hour, Date, Place	Summary of Events and Information	Remarks and references to Appendices
July 1917		
Dragon Camp. Cont⁴ 27th	units & to prepare to move off at two notes.	
Map ref. A15.4.5.7. Sheet 28 28th	Heavy bombardment continues. Heavy demand made on Corps RE Park for supply of Bent slabs for making forward Roads and completing Causeways across the Yser Canal to enemy Take "Tanks."	
29th	Tanks passed over Maringo Causeway during the night 28/29th. Result satisfactory. Pontoons passed forward to forward transport lines. Pontoons for Cactus Pontoon to be embarked aft. Zero. Pontoons etc. for construction of Pontoon bridge across Yser Canal before Zero, and forward to Canal Bank during the night of 29/30th. Due to the heavy rain the onwards transport roads were not passable. (X day)	
Eludenigh Chateau 6 Pm 30th	Heavy rain continues, enformously weather for operations. D.W.H. Bn moves forward to B.H.G. Headquarters at 6pm (L. Evening, CinC) (Y day) Final preparation being made for the attack on the Enemy at Zero hour tomorrow morning.	

WAR DIARY
or
INTELLIGENCE SUMMARY.
(Erase heading not required.)

Army Form C. 2118.

Page 11

Hour, Date, Place	Summary of Events and Information	Remarks and references to Appendices
Forward Batt Div HQ at Elverdinghe Chateau Sheet 28 B.14.c.2.1. July 31, 17	The attack was launched at 3:50 A.M. The 38th Div formary as follows, with left a line running from B.12. Central to U.22. Central, and the right a line running from C.14 Central to Jolie Farm and U.29. Central. The centre of attack crossing the River Steenbeek at U.28 Central. Guards Division on the left and 51st Division (Highland) on the right. The objective consisting of four Courses, viz: 1st Blue Line, 2nd Black line, 3rd Green line & "Green Dotted Line." Enemy on the River Steenbeek. 124 Field Co RE detailed to work on Strong Points on the Blue and Black Lines. 123 Field Co RE for work on the Green Line and the 151st Field Co RE for work on Bridges crossing the Yser Canal. Lt A.H. Souter RE 123 70 Co RE in charge of all work on forward roads between Yser Canal & Huidelstein Road. Blue line captured at 5-0 A.M. Black line captured 5-45 A.M. Green line captured 8-0 A.M. Green dotted line at 9-30 A.M.	

WAR DIARY or INTELLIGENCE SUMMARY

Army Form C. 2118

Aug 1917

Place	Date	Hour	Summary of Events and Information	Remarks and references to Appendices
38 Div HQ 11 Batt HQ Elverdinghe Statⁿ Pdt 28 B.n.E.H.	July 31st	(Continued) Battⁿ	The 11th K.R.R. with D.A.H. Soutar R.E. in charge of work. cleared a track to the rite from Marengo Causeway, for artillery. Difficulties were experienced in moving the guns over the open ground east of Canal Bank before any rain had fallen. Buck sleds were used for towing the carriages across the marsh. Artillery used the track during the day. 123 and 124 Field Co^s R.E. continued work during the day consolidating and improving the Strong Points on the Blue, Black and Green Lines. 151 Field Co. R.E. continued work on Bridges, repairs & maintenance, and cutting approaches through Canal Bank for Cactus Pontoon Bridge.	

Geo. Morgan
Capt & a/Ajt R.E.
To CRE 38 Division

Secret.

Original

War Diary

August 1917

C.R.E. 38th Division

Vol 20

Army Form C. 2118.

WAR DIARY
or
INTELLIGENCE SUMMARY.
(Erase heading not required.)

Instructions regarding War Diaries and Intelligence Summaries are contained in F.S. Regs., Part II. and the Staff Manual respectively. Title pages will be prepared in manuscript.

Hour, Date, Place	Summary of Events and Information	Remarks and references to Appendices
August 1917		
Sluerighe Chat".	Right Division, Left Corps. Ypres Salient.	
Map ref. Sheet 28 B.14.b.2.1.	1st Field Coy RE and Pioneers employed pushing forward tramways, Plinks and Duckboard Tracks over the ground gained, also improving defence works.	
	2nd ditto.	
Dragon Camp. Map ref. Sheet 28 A.15.6.5.7.	3rd Divl HQrs moved South. Rear Headquarters and preparations made to relief by 20th Division. Corps RE Pioneers employed as above, also work on stepping forward Dumps for offensive operations of 20th Div.	
	4th as above.	
	5th as above. 1st & 3rd CoyRE relieved by 84 Field CoyRE	
	6th 38th Div relieved by 20th (Light) Division.	
	7th Headquarters moved to Central Camp Proven. 157 Field CoyRE relieved by 96 Field CoyRE. 123 Field CoyRE employed when Chief Engineer XIV Corps require in forward area.	

WAR DIARY
or
INTELLIGENCE SUMMARY.

(Erase heading not required.)

Army Form C. 2118.

Instructions regarding War Diaries and Intelligence Summaries are contained in F. S. Regs., Part II. and the Staff Manual respectively. Title pages will be prepared in manuscript.

Hour, Date, Place	Summary of Events and Information	Remarks and references to Appendices
August 8th	124 Field C. RE commenced work on Corps tramway. Balance 157 Field C. RE resting.	
9th	Div. at reserve at Proven.	
10th	do	
11th	do	
12th	do	
13th	do	
14th	do	
15th	do	
16th	do	
17th	do	
18th	Preparations made for relieving 20th (Light) Division.	
19th	Div. Headquarters moved to Elverdinghe Chateau and relieved 20th (Light) Division.	
20th	123 Field C. RE commenced work on new Div. Headquarters Camp. 124 Field C. RE employed on forward tramway and RE Dumps. 157 Field C. RE employed on forward roads and tracks, also communication trench from Pilkem Rd, Steenbeek.	

WAR DIARY
or
INTELLIGENCE SUMMARY

Army Form C. 2118

Place	Date	Hour	Summary of Events and Information	Remarks and references to Appendices
Elverdinghe Chateau	August 1917 20/8/17		Pioneers and party of 157 Field Co RE employed on Green Line digging trenches and wiring etc.	
	21st		123 Field Co RE taken off work on new Bde HQ and sent forward to work on Green Line defences.	
	22nd		Work continues as above.	
	23rd		do	
	24		do	
	25		do	
	26		do	
	27		do	
	28		do	
	29		do	
	30		do	
	31		do	

JR Morgan
Lieut Colonel RE
to CRE 38 Divn

Secret

Original War Diary
September 1917.

Headquarters Royal Engineers
38th Division

1-10-17

Vol 21

Army Form C. 2118

WAR DIARY
or
INTELLIGENCE SUMMARY
(Erase heading not required.)

Headquarters.
Royal Engineers.
38th Division.

Page 1.

Instructions regarding War Diaries and Intelligence Summaries are contained in F.S. Regs., Part II. and the Staff Manual respectively. Title Pages will be prepared in manuscript.

Place	Date	Hour	Summary of Events and Information	Remarks and references to Appendices
ELVERDINGHE CHATEAU				
SEPT.	1st		R.E. Headquarters at Advanced Divisional Headquarters, ELVERDINGHE CHATEAU. Field Companies employed improving consolidated points and pushing forward communication trenches, and making gun roads for further offensive operations.	
	2nd		Work continued as for 1st. Lieut Col. B.S.Phillpotts. D.S.O. C.R.E. 38th Division, wounded near LANGEMARCK.	
	3rd		Work as for 2nd. Major J.C.I.Wood R.E. commanding 123rd Field Co. R.E. assumed duty as C.R.E.	
	4th		Work as above. Lt. Col. B.S.Phillpotts. D.S.O. C.R.E. 38th Division, Died of Wounds at 47.CCS.	
	5th		Work as above. Lt. Col. B.S.Phillpotts. D.S.O. buried in the Cemetery at No. 47. C.C.S.	
	6th		Continued work as above.	
	7th		do do	
	8th		Lieut. L.E.Kelsall. D.S.O assumed duties as C.R.E. 38th Division.	
	9th		151st Field Co. R.E relieved by Field Co. R.E. 20th Division.	
	10th		123rd Field Co. R.E relieved by Field Co. R.E. 20th Division.	
	11th		124th Field Co. R.E relieved by Field Co. R.E. 20th Division. 38th (Welsh) Division relieved by 20th (Light Division. Relief completed by 10.am. Divisional H.Q. moved to Central Camp., PROVEN.	
PROVEN.	12th		Div. H.Q. at Proven.	
	13th		Div. H.Q. moved from Proven to Estairs,(XIth Corps.)	
	14th		Div. H.Q. at Estairs, pending relief of 57th Division.	
	15th		At Estairs.	
	16th		124th Field Co. RME relieved Field Co. R.E of 57th Division in the FLEURBAIX sector. 151st Field Co. R.E. relieved Field Co. R.E of 57th Division in the ARMENTIERES sector.	
Croix Du Bac	17th		38th Division relieved 57th Division 123rd Field Co. R.E. relieved Field Co. R.E. 57th Division in Bois Grenier, Sector. G.O.C. 38th (Welsh) Division assumed command of Armentieres, Bois Grenier, and Fleurbaix Sectors.	
	18th		Field Coys. R.E continued work of maintenance etc as handed over by 57th Division.	
	19th		Work as above	
	20th		do do	
	21st		do do	
	22nd		do do	
	23rd		do do	

Army Form C. 2118

WAR DIARY
or
INTELLIGENCE SUMMARY
(Erase heading not required.)

Page II

Instructions regarding War Diaries and Intelligence Summaries are contained in F.S. Regs., Part II. and the Staff Manual respectively. Title Pages will be prepared in manuscript.

Place	Date	Hour	Summary of Events and Information	Remarks and references to Appendices
CROIX DU BAC.	24th		Work as for 23rd.	
	25th		do do	
	26th		do do inspection of	
	27th		Completion of all Infantry and A.S.C wagon lines with "Q" branch. The condition generally found very bad and large amount of work necessary to make the places habitable for the winter.	
	28th		Work as above.	
	29th		Three Sections of R.E (one from each Field Coy.) detailed for work on wagon lines in Back Area.	
	30th		Heavy demands made on C.R.E. Corps Troops for necessary R.E.Material required to make wagon lines habitable for the winter.	

J.E.Evans.
Lieut. Col.
C.R.E. 38th (Welsh) Division.

S E C R E T.

Copy. No. _____

C.R.E. 38th (Welsh) Division Order No. 37.

9th Sept. 1917.

1. The 38th (Welsh) Division (less Artillery) will be relieved by the 20th (Light) Division (less Artillery) between the 9th and 11th September.

2. The 151st Field Coy. R.E. will be relieved on the 9th Sept. by the 96th Field Co. R.E. Relief to be completed by 9.am 9th inst.
The 151st Field Co. R.E (less Transport and cyclists) will entrain at 1.30.pm 9th inst at ELVERDINGHE, and detrain at PROVEN for P.5. Area.
Transport and cyclists will proceed by road.

3. The 123rd Field Co. R.E. will be relieved on the 10th Sept by the 84th Field Co. R.E. Relief to be completed by 9.am 10th inst.
The 123rd Field Co. R.E will proceed by road from Cardoen Farm to PHEASANT CAMP, Sheet 27.F.5.c.4.5.

4. The 124th Field Co. R.E will be relieved on the 11th Sept by the 83rd Field Co. R.E. but will move to CARDOEN FARM on the evening of the 10th inst, taking over Billets from the 123rd Field Co. R.E. On the 11th inst, the 124th Field Co. R.E will proceed by road to P.1. Area, PROVEN.

5. Movements by road will be accordance with Fifth Army Traffic Regulations. Units moving by train must arrive at entraining station half an hour before the time the train is due to start.

6. Advance parties from 20th Divnl. R.E consisting of 1 officer and 6.O.R from each Field Coy, will report to O.C. Coys being relieved by 6.pm 8th inst to 151 Field Co and 6.pm 9th inst for 123rd and 124th Field Coys.
All plans and documents relating to work in hand or proposed, also motor cycles, aeroplane photographs and trench maps, will be handed to relieving unit and receipts obtained.

7. Field Coys R.E will arrange to recover their Pontoon Equipment which was left at the 151 Coys billet, PROVEN, as soon as possible after arrival in the PROVEN Area.

8. C.R.E. 20th (Light) Division will take over 38th Div. R.E Park and workshops, Ondank, at noon 10th inst.
Lieut G.Smith. R.E, Oi/c. Park, will return the party of attached Infantry to their Units on the evening of the 10th inst. The R.F.Section, 123rd Coy, and party of 19th Pioneers will also return to their Units on the evening of the 10th inst.

9. Completion of all moves, with locations of Coy. Hd.Qrs. will be reported to this office by wire.

(1)

10. C.R.E. Office, 38th (Welsh) Division will close at ELVERDINGHE CHATEAU on the morning of the 11th inst and will open at 10.am on the same day at PROVEN, (Sheet 27. F.7.b.5.1).

11. Acknowledge.

Issued at 1.pm.

Captain. R.E.
Adjutant, R.E. 38th (Welsh) Division

Copies to:-

O.C. 123rd Field Coy. R.E.
O.C. 124th Field Coy. R.E.
O.C. 151st Field Coy. R.E.
C.R.E. 20th Division.
38th Div. G.S.
38th Div. Q.
C.E. XIVth Corps.
O.C. 19th Welsh Regt.
S.S.O.
Div. Train.
A.D.V.S.
A.D.M.S.
O.i/c. 38th Div. R.E.Park.
Fil=.
Signals.

SECRET.   Copy No. 9

C.R.E. 38th (Welsh) Division Order No. 39.

10th Sept. 1917.

Ref. Maps:

Information.

The 38th (Welsh) Division (less Artillery) will relieve the 57th (West Lancashire) Division (less Artillery) between the 15th and 17th September.

1. Field Companies R.E will move from the PROVEN AREA with Brigade Groups, in the following order:-

   <u>113 Brigade.</u>   <u>114 Brigade.</u>   <u>115 Brigade.</u>
   123rd Field Co. R.E. 124th Field Co. R.E. 151st Field Co. R.E.

2. Moves will be carried out in accordance with the attached March Table.

3. The 123rd Field Co. R.E, with attached Infantry, will relieve the 505 Field Co. R.E in the BOIS GRENIER Area on the 17th Sept.
   Billets for Hd.Qrs and four Sections and attached Infantry will be at the Farm adjoining the EQUINGHEM LAUNDRY at H.5.a.25.55. Horse Lines will be at TROIS TILLEULS, at B.28.b.1.5.
   Relief will not commence till 3.pm.

4. The 124th Field Co. R.E, with attached Infantry, will relieve the 421 Field Co. R.E in the FLEURBAIX Area on the 16th inst.
   Billets for Hd.Qrs and four sections will be at PORT a CLOUSE Farm, H.21.a.10.99. Horse lines will be at BAC ST MAUR. G.18.d.2.5.
   Relief not to commence till 3.pm.

5. The 151st Field Co. R.E, and attached Infantry, will relieve the 502 Field Co. R.E in the ARMENTIERES Area on the 16th inst. Billets for Hd.Qrs and 2 Sections will be in RUE SADI CARNOT, Armentieres, C.25.c.45.32.
   Billets for 2 sections at HOUPLINES, C.27.a.9.8. Horse Lines at TROIS TILLEULS, at B.28.b.1.5.
   Relief to be completed by 5.pm.

6. Each Field Coy. R.E will send advance parties by road, as follows:-
   123rd Field Co. R.E, 2. Officers & 12. O.R (cyclists) to report to O.C. 505 Field Co. R.E on 13th inst.
   124th Field Co. R.E, 2 Officers and 12 O.R to report to O.C. 421 Field Co. R.E on the 12th inst.
   151st Field Co. R.E., 2 Officers and 12 O.R to report to O.C. 502 Field Co. R.E on the 12th inst.

7. O.i/c. 38th Divnl. R.E.Park, (2nd Lieut G.Smith. R.E) with R.S.M and 4. O.R will report to O.i/c. 57th Divn. R.E.Park BAC ST MAUR on the 14th inst. Relief (R.E & loading parties) will be completed by 10.am 17th inst.

SECRET.

9. The following will be detailed to report to O.i/c.Divnl. R.E. Park, BAC ST MAUR, at 9.am 17th inst for work at Divisional Workshops, and will be rationed by C.R.E. 38th Division, from 18th inclusive:-

123rd Field Co. R.E.	124th Field Co. R.E.	151st Field Co. R.E.
1 Carpenter	1 Carpenter	1 Carpenter (N.C.O)
1 Plumber or Tinsmith.	1 Fitter.	1 Fitter.
1 Blacksmith.	1 Blacksmith.	1 Blacksmith.
1 Painter	1 Mason	1 Painter.

O.C. 19th Pioneers will detail 1 Sergeant and 12 O.R.

In addition to above, 1 Officer and 50 O.R. Infantry, will be detailed from 38th Division on 16th inst, to relieve the loading party now supplied from 57th Division for work at Divisional R.E.Park.

10. R.E. advance parties should report at Field Co. R.E wagon lines and obtain guides before proceeding to the forward area. They may also have to arrange for extra billets for attached Infantry.
Horses should not be taken into ARMENTIERES.

11. Field Coys. R.E will take over all work in hand, all maps plans, documents etc of work in hand, or proposed, but will not complete the reliefs before the times stated.
Completion of reliefs will be wired to C.R.E. 38th Division.

12. C.R.E's Office, 38th Division, will close at Central Camp, PROVEN, on the 13th inst and open the same day at ETAIRES, and will close at ETAIRES on the 17th inst and re-open at CROIX DU BAC on the same day at 10.am.

Acknowledge.

Capt. R.E.
Adjutant R.E. 38th Divisional
Engineers.

Issued at;
Copies to; O.C. 123rd Field Co. R.E.
O.C. 124th Field Co. R.E.
O.C. 151st Field Co. R.E.
O.C. 19th Welsh Regt.
G.S. 38th Division.
"Q" 38th Division.
38th Signals.
S.S.O. 38th Division.
Div. Train.
D.A.D.V.S.
A.D.M.S.
O.i/c. 38th Div. R.E.Park.
C.R.E. 57th Division.
File.

Army Form W.3091.

Cover for Documents.

SECRET

Vol 22

Nature of Enclosures.

War Diaries.
38th
Divisional
Engineers

October 1917

Notes, or Letters written.

Army Form C. 2118.

WAR DIARY
or
INTELLIGENCE SUMMARY.
(Erase heading not required.)

Headquarters, Royal Engineers, 38th (Welsh) Division.
October, 1917.
(2 sheets. sheet 1.)

Instructions regarding War Diaries and Intelligence Summaries are contained in F.S. Regs., Part II. and the Staff Manual respectively. Title pages will be prepared in manuscript.

Hour, Date, Place	Summary of Events and Information	Remarks and references to Appendices

CROIX DU BAC.

1st to 31st.

R.E., H.Q. remained at CROIX DU BAC during the month. The 3 Field Companies (less 1 section each, working O.R.E. direct, in back area assisting Units with repair and reconstruction of horse lines), continued under C.R.E. in their respective brigade areas, as last month. Work was chiefly concentrated on drainage, O.P's, Concrete dugouts &c for various purposes, repair and renewal of Screening, revetting communication trenches, and making certain trench mortar emplacements requiring technical skill. In addition R.E. assistance was given to Infantry, Artillery &c for work which they were carrying out (e.g. revetting trenches, making dugouts, making trench mortar emplacements &c.)

2/Lieut. PHILLIPS of 19th Welsh Regt. (Pioneers) was appointed Divisional Tramway Officer on tramlines in the Divisional area. The remainder of the Pioneers (less some in R.E. Divisional Workshops) were employed on the following two jobs, (A) making a new Communication trench with firebays from WINDY POST (Sheet 36. N.2.b.2.3.) to Support line at sheet 36. N.8.b.1.4., so as to form a defensive flank facing S.W. (B) making a defensive switch facing N.E., to connect the Support line at CITY POST (Sheet 36. H.36. central) to the subsidiary line at sheet 36. H.30.a.7.1.)

The Support line is the main line of defence as far N.E. as CITY POST ; beyond that the subsidiary line becomes the main line of defence. Hence the necessity for the switch. The route followed by the switch is by CITY ROAD to H.36.a.4.6., thence along OLD CUT to where it meets GREATWOOD AVENUE at H.30.d.5.0. and then back along GREATWOOD AVENUE to the subsidiary line.

Headquarters,   Royal Engineers,   Army Form C. 2118.

WAR DIARY
or
INTELLIGENCE SUMMARY.

38th (Welsh) Division.

October, 1917.   (Sheets 2. Sheet 2.)

(Erase heading not required.)

Instructions regarding War Diaries and Intelligence Summaries are contained in F.S. Regs., Part II. and the Staff Manual respectively. Title pages will be prepared in manuscript.

Hour, Date, Place	Summary of Events and Information	Remarks and references to Appendices
	Continued.	
	On taking over the area from the 57th Division in September, 1917, the Divisional R.E. Dumps and Workshops were at BAC ST MAUR and ERQUINGHEM, and these were continued by the 38th Division. There were too many forward R.E. Dumps, and during October these were reduced to 2 each for the ARMENTIERES and FLEURBAIX sectors, and 4 for the BOIS GRENIER Sector. On 17th October the R.E. Dump at BAC ST MAUR was shelled and on one or two subsequent occasions bombed. No serious damage or casualties were caused on any of these occasions, beyond some of the civilian workmen and women being frightened away. There was a good deal of rain during the month, with some consequent flooding of trenches.	

T.S.Kercoll
Lieut. Colonel, R.E.
Commanding Royal Engineer, 38th Division.

WAR DIARY or INTELLIGENCE SUMMARY

(Erase heading not required.)

Army Form C. 2118

Headquarters, R.E.
38th Division.
November 1917. (/ Sheet.)

Vol 23

Place	Date	Hour	Summary of Events and Information	Remarks and references to Appendices
CROIX DU BAC.	1st – 30th.		Work was continued during the month by Field Companies and Pioneers on the same lines as during October. "C" Company 19th Welsh Regt. (Pioneers) was moved into the ARMENTIERES Sector and started work there on the 4th. On 18th November 1917 "B" Company Pioneers was moved away to an unknown destination for special work and 2nd Lieut. H.L.Davies (Divisional Pioneers) was appointed Divisional Tramway Officer vice 2nd Lieut. Phillips who belongs to "B" Company. On 28th C.R.E. ordered the work by Pioneers on defensive flank between WINDY POST and support line (see October diary) to cease. The work was not complete, but certain definite lengths of it were, and the defensive switch from CITY POST (see October diary) was considered more important, and orders were issued for the men to assist the work there. On 22nd the 38th Division came under XVth Corps which relieved XIth Corps. Orders were received 29/11/17 that the R.E.Dump and workshops BAC ST MAUR were to be given up, the owner having claimed that the shelling and consequent damage to his factory, in the yard of which the dump and workshops are, which occurred in October, were due to the presence of the dump. A site for the new workshops was provisionally chosen on 30/11/17 at G.17.a. Sheet 36. The proposal is to build workshops here, as it seems a quiet and well screened spot, and to use the present dump and shops at ERQUINGHEM chiefly as a dump and issuing yard.	

Reeves.

Lieut. Colonel, R.E.
Commanding Royal Engineers, 38th Division.

Army Form C. 2118

WAR DIARY or INTELLIGENCE SUMMARY

(Erase heading not required.)

Headquarters, R.E.
38th Division.
December 1917.

Remarks and references to Appendices: WD 24

Place	Date	Hour	Summary of Events and Information
CROIX DU BAC.	2nd.		R.E. Headquarters continued to remain at CROIX DU BAC during the month. Work in connection with the XVth Corps Conference policy of 4' concrete constructions for machine gun dugouts, Company Headquarters and Battalion Headquarters, and wiring to be increased in depth, was put in hand.
	10th		On 10th December C.E.P. 2nd Division C.E.P. visited the different works then in hand by 38th Division R.E's preparatory to handing over.
	11th		The 124th Field Company, R.E. moved to ARMENTIERES (Jute Factory) and took over all work then being done or supervised by the 151st Field Company, R.E. in the Right Sub-section of the Left Sub- Brigade Area. The 151st Field Company, R.E. on being relieved, took up work in the Left Sub-section of the Left Brigade. Move commenced of the R.E. Park from BAC ST MAUR to LA BOUDRELLE. THE SITE PROVISIONALLY SELECTED on the 30th 11/1917 at G.17.a. Sheet 36. This move was completed on the 14th inst. and new workshops and roads were put in hand for construction.
	19th		The Left Brigade Area and half of the 113th Brigade Area was handed over to the 3rd Australian Division, works then in hand were inspected by Acting C.R.E. and Acting C.R.E., 3rd Australian Division.
	20th		151st Field Company, R.E. were relieved in the ARMENTIERES Sector by the 9th Australian Field Company and handed over all schemes in that Sector preparatory to move to NOUVEAU MONDE for work on the FLEURBAIX defences. The 124th Field Company, R.E. vacated billets and moved to billets occupied by the 130th Field Ambulance SAILLY and took over work in the FLEURBAIX Section from the R.E's 2nd Division C.E.P.
	21st		123rd Field Company, R.E. were relieved in the Left Sub-section of the BOIS GRENIER Section by the 11th Australian Field Company and handed over all schemes and works and moved to billets occupied by 130th Field Ambulance at SAILLY to commence work in the 113th Brigade Area to PARK ROW, TIN BARN TRAMWAY, taking over TIN BARN AREA) to GREATWOOD AVENUE from the 124th Field Company, R.E.
	27th		2 Companies of the 12th Divisional Pioneers (5th Northamptonshire Regt.) reported for work on the Subsidiary Line Posts. On the 28th inst. Acting C.R.E. with Officers from these Companies reconnoitred the work in project.
	30th		"B" Company, 19th Welsh Pioneers returned to the 38th Division for work. Major Wood, O.C. 123rd Field Company, R.E. has been acting C.R.E. during the absence of Lieut. Colonel T.E.Kelsall, D.S.O., R.E., C.R.E., whilst on special leave to England.

Wood
Major, R.E.
a/C.R.E., 38th Division.

Army Form C. 2118.

Headquarters,
Royal Engineers,
38th Division.
January 1918.

WAR DIARY
or
INTELLIGENCE SUMMARY
(Erase heading not required.)

Instructions regarding War Diaries and Intelligence Summaries are contained in F.S. Regs., Part II. and the Staff Manual respectively. Title Pages will be prepared in manuscript.

Place	Date	Hour	Summary of Events and Information	Remarks and references to Appendices
CROIX DU BAC.	1st-14th.		R.E. Headquarters remained at CROIX DU BAC.	
	1st.		The troops working under C.R.E. and the work they were on, were as follows :- 123rd Field Coy. in Left Brigade (BOIS GRENIER) Sector. 124th Field Coy. in Right Brigade (FLEURBAIX) Sector. 151st Field Coy. on FLEURBAIX Village defences. 19th Welsh Regt.(Pioneers) 1 Coy. on Right Flank Defence (i.e. on line connecting subsidiary line at WINDY POST, with support line in front.) 1 Company working under O.C. 151st Field Coy. R.E. 1 Coy. on CITY SWITCH (i.e. a line connecting support line at CITY POST with subsidiary line at CROMBAJOT) 1 Coy. on tramway maintenance and on the improvement of BOIS GRENIER defences etc. 2 Coys. 5th Northampton Regt. (Pioneers 12th Division) on improving posts in the subsidiary line from CROIX BLANCHE POST to CHARRED POST. 90 men of XVth Corps Cyclists) Working under O.C. 151st Field Coy. R.E. 176 M.G. Coy. 38th Division)	
	13th		124 Field Coy. R.E. was relieved by 87th Field Coy. R.E. of 12th Division, so as to be available for work under C.R.E., 38th Division on a new defensive line to be constructed on the left bank of the River LYS between BEAUPRE (West of LA GORGUE) and PONT DE NIEPPE. C.R.E. and O.C. 124th Field Coy. R.E. made a preliminary reconnaissance of this line.	
	15th		38th Division was relieved in line by 12th Division, and Divisional and R.E. Headquarters moved from CROIX DU BAC to MERVILLE. On relief, 123rd and 151st Field Coys. R.E. and 38th Divisional Pioneers remained behind under orders of C.R.E., 12th Division. C.R.E., 38th Division came under C.E. XVth Corps for work on the new LYS line.	
	16th		123rd and 151st Field Coys. R.E. and 2 Coys. 19th Welsh Regt. (Pioneers) were replaced by corresponding units of 12th Division, and came under the orders of C.R.E., XVth Corps Troops, for work.	
	15th-31st.		R.E. Headquarters remained at MERVILLE, and C.R.E., with 124th Field Coy. R.E. worked on LYS	

WAR DIARY (Continued) Sheet 2.
or
INTELLIGENCE SUMMARY January 1918.

(Erase heading not required.)

Army Form C. 2118

Place	Date	Hour	Summary of Events and Information	Remarks and references to Appendices
	22nd		line with Infantry working parties from all three Divisions of XVth Corps, viz: 12th, 38th and 57th. The first infantry party started work on the 20th, and before the end of the month, parties up to over 1400 were working daily. A party of 1 Officer and 30 Other Ranks 3rd Australian Tunnelling Coy. arrived at PONT DE NIEPPE for special work under C.R.E., and started work next day. The weather in the early part of the month was cold, with alternate snow, thaw, frost and rain. The last few days were, however, mild and bright.	

J.C. Mead.

Lieutenant-Colonel, R.E.,
Commanding Royal Engineers, 38th Division.
1st February 1918.

Army Form C. 2118
Sheet 1.

WAR DIARY
or
INTELLIGENCE SUMMARY

(Erase heading not required.)

Headquarters,
Royal Engineers,
38th (Welsh) Division.

February, 1918.

Vol 26

Place	Date	Hour	Summary of Events and Information	Remarks and references to Appendices
MERVILLE.	1st–15th.		R.E.Hd. Qrs at MERVILLE. C.R.E. and 124 Field Coy R.E. working under C.E., XVth Corps on the LYS Line, 123 and 151 Field Coys R.E. and 2 Coys 19th Welsh Regt. (Pioneers) working under C.R.E. XVth Corps Troops, and 2 Coys 19th Welsh Regt. (Pioneers) working under C.R.E., 12th Division, all as at end of January.	
STEENWERCK.	16th.		38th Division relieved 57th Division in line (WEZ MACQUART, ARMENTIERES and HOUPLINES sectors) with all 3 Field Coys and Pioneers, C.R.E., 57th Division taking over from C.R.E., 38th Division the work on the LYS Line and the work of Det. 3rd Australian Tunnelling Coy., (their strength had been increased to about 60, during February). R.E.,H.Qrs 38th Division moved same day from MERVILLE to STEENWERCK.	C.R.E's Order No. 45
			As soon as the 38th Division had taken over, Infantry Brigadiers were made responsible for all work in their areas from RUE FLEURIE Switch–CROSS CUT–Eastern defences of HOUPLINES inclusive forward; behind that C.R.E. was made responsible. To assist Infantry Brigadiers, each had one section of its affiliated Field Coy placed under its orders for technical work.	
			151 Field Coy worked on right and gave one section to 115 Infty. Brigade, in WEZ MACQUART sector; 123 Field Coy worked in centre, and gave one section to 113 Infty. Brigade in ARMENTIERES sector+attached. 124 Field Coy worked on left and gave one section to 114 Infty. Brigade in HOUPLINES sector. C.R.E., XVth Corps Troops worked under orders of 38th Division in the right portion of the area for which C.R.E., 38th Division was responsible, having having under him two Field Coys of 57th Division, whom he employed on making shell proof shelters for M.G. detachments; he also did wiring with their attached infantry. This arrangement was still in force at the end of February. When 38th Division went into line, 1 Coy Pioneers was placed under the orders of 114 Infty. Bde. for a specific piece of work; the other 3 Coys were at first placed under orders of C.R.E.,XVth Corps Troops for work on new trenches in same area, as he was doing work as in above. On 21/2/1918 the Pioneers were reorganized in three companies instead of four; 1 remained with 114 Infty. Bde., 1 worked on trenches in area of 123 Field Coy and 1 on trenches in area of 124 Field Coy RME. the last two under orders of C.R.E. 38th Division. The work of Field Coys was the construction of a trench system along general line of L'ARMEE switch and a continuation of this northwards east of ARMENTIERES and NOUVEL HOUPLINES to the LYS. Also shell proof reinforced concrete shelters of Hd. Qrs and for M.G. teams. In each Infty. Bde, 1 Battn. was in reserve, and the bulk of these were available for work on the	

Army Form C. 2118
Sheet 2.

WAR DIARY
or
INTELLIGENCE SUMMARY
(Erase heading not required.)

Instructions regarding War Diaries and Intelligence Summaries are contained in F. S. Regs., Part II. and the Staff Manual respectively. Title Pages will be prepared in manuscript.

Place	Date	Hour	Summary of Events and Information	Remarks and references to Appendices
			on the same line.	
			During February the weather was generally good.	

T. Geenae.
Lieut.Col. R.E.
Commanding Royal Engineer, 38th Division.
1st March, 1918.

Vol 27

March 1918

War Diaries

38 Divn
R.E.

C.R.E.,
38th (WELSH)
DIVISION.
No.
Date 3/4/18

Headquarters, R.E. Army Form C. 2118
38th (Welsh) Division.

WAR DIARY
or
INTELLIGENCE SUMMARY
March 1918.

(Erase heading not required.)

Instructions regarding War Diaries and Intelligence Summaries are contained in F.S. Regs., Part II. and the Staff Manual respectively. Title Pages will be prepared in manuscript.

Place	Date	Hour	Summary of Events and Information	Remarks and references to Appendices
STEENWERCK	1st to 31st		R.E. H.Qrs. at STEENWERCK. The arrangements for work were the same as at the end of February, except that on 20th March the two Field Companies of 57th Division working under C.R.E., XVth Corps Troops were replaced by two Field Companies of 12th Division: the latter were withdrawn a few days later owing to situation further South, and C.R.E., XVth Corps Troops handed over to C.R.E., 38th Division the work they had been doing. Orders were received during the latter part of the month to have twelve light floating bridges ready to put across the River LYS in case of necessity at selected sites. These were all ready in the Divisional R.E. Yard at ERQUINGHEM by the end of the month, but owing to the 38th Division receiving orders to move, it was not possible to prepare the sites. On 28/3/18 orders were received for the Division to be ready to move. On 29/3/18 C.R.E. 34th Division came reference taking over. On 30/3/18 C.R.E., 34th Division took over. Orders are for Division to move 31/3/18, some of the units having already moved.	Sketch of floating bridge & schedule of stores attached

T. E. Evans.

Lieut. Col. R.E.,
Commanding Royal Engineers, 38th (Welsh) Division.
30th March 1918.

—ELEVATION—

—PLAN—

—SKETCH OF FLOAT BRIDGE—

Scale (about) ⅛" = 1'-0"

Schedule of principal stores - 4 Raft Bridge

No.	Stores.	Reference to map.	Remarks.
8.	Floats.	A.	Two per raft.
2.	" 15'0"	B.	Single float for shore bay.
12.	4"x 3"-Road bearers	C.	On rafts.
6.	do. 5'2" Road bearers	D.	On shore float.
6.	do. 7'6" " "	E.	Shore bay.
4.	Sets 1" decking.	F.	For rafts.
2.	" "	G.	Shore float and ba
10.	Timber clamps with bolts and nuts.	H.	For connecting rafts.
1.	Steel cable.	K.	1 spare length provided.
5.	15' lengths rope	L.	Tie rope.
1.	Length rope about 100'	-	For swinging bridg
12.	Anchor Pickets.	M.	
	Spun yarn.		100 feet.
	Stores for one raft.		
2.	Floats.		
3.	4" x 3" - 15'0" Rd. bearers		These will be required when brid consists of more than 4 rafts.
1.	Set 1" decking.		
1.	15'0" length rope.		
2.	Timber clamps with bolts and nuts.		

SPECIFICATION.

General. The float bridge shewn on sketch, spans a water way o 79' and consists of :-

    4 rafts each 15'0" long.
    2 shore bays and floats each 12'9" long.

Span adjustment. The adjustment of length of bridge to suit the width of waterway to be done as follows :-

1. By increasing or decreasing the number of rafts.
2. By varying the shore span from 1' to 6' the normal span being 4' as shewn on sketch.
3. By : selecting a more suitable width of waterway say, within 20 or 30 yards of site. It is not desirable that banks should be cut.

    Reference No. 2, the clear span of shore bay for unif loading on float should be 4' if possible, the same as the span between floats on raft. When the shore span is only about 1' care must be taken against float grounding on fall o water level.

    Should the above methods not meet the case a special raft will require to be made.

SECRET.

C.R.E., 38th Division.

ORDER 46.

INFORMATION.

1.   34th Division will relieve 38th Division in the Left Section of XVth Corps Front, with the exception of the R.A.

2.   Reliefs of Field Coys. R.E. will be as follows :-

      123rd Field Coy. will be relieved by 208 Field Coy.
      124th Field Coy. "   "   "   " 207   "   "
      151st Field Coy. "   "   "   " 209   "   "

123rd Field Coy. R.E. will move out to DOULIEU tomorrow morning taking with them all documents, demolition schemes, maps etc. and are due to arrive at this place by 1 p.m. A guide will be sent to meet lorries with Pontoons at DOULIEU Church at 1 p.m. O.C. 123rd Field Coy. will then arrange offloading and loading on to 123 Coy's Pontoon and trestle wagons

38th Division Field Coys. will at once prepare handing over notes of work in hand and proposed.

3. Advance parties.

An advanced party will be coming up from 34th Division tomorrow afternoon 30th inst. by lorry, details of which are shewn below:-

Party of 208 Field Coy. R.E. (including C.O., 1 N.C.O. and 1 O.R.) will be at DOULIEU Church about 3.30. p.m. 30/3/1918. A guide from 123rd Field Coy. to be at DOULIEU Church at 3.20 p.m. and wait for lorry. C.Officer will get out of lorry and take over all papers etc. from O.C. 123rd Field Coy. R.E. The N.C.O. and 1 O.R. will go forward with the lorry and will take over billets from 1 N.C.O. and 1 O.R. of 123rd Field Coy. R.E. left behind for that purpose, the latter will afterwards proceed by bicycle to DOULIEU to rejoin their Company.

O i/c R.E.Park will detail a guide to be at road junction B.27.d.2.8. at 3.45. p.m. and wait for lorry to take R.S.M., 34th Division to R.E. Park ERQUINGHEM where he will remain.

Party of 209 Field Coy. R.E. (C.O., 1 Officer and 1 O.R.) will proceed with lorry to Railway Crossing at B.28.b.2.7., where a guide from 151st Field Coy. R.E. will meet them. Guide to be there at 4 p.m. and await until lorry will arrive. The 209 Coy. party will remain at 151st Field Coy. Billets and C.O. will take over from C.O. 151st Field Coy. all documents, demolition schemes maps etc

Party of 207 Field Coy. R.E. (1 C.O., 1 Officer and 1 O.R.) will be at Railway Crossing B.28 . B.2.7., where a guide from 124th Field Coy. R.E. will meet them. Guide to be there at 4 p.m. and await until the lorry will arrive. The guide will arrange to leave the party of 1 N.C.O. and 1 O.R. of 208 Field Coy. R.E. at the billets of 123rd Field Coy. R.E. PONT DE NIEPPE and then proceed to Coy. H.Q. 124th Field Coy. at Rue Sadi Carnot ARMENTIERES. 207 Field Coy. R.E. party will remain at 124th

Field Coy. R.E. billets and will arrange with O.C. 124th Field Coy. R.E. to take over all documents demolition schemes maps etc. O.C. 207 Field Coy. R.E. will give instructions as to disposal of lorry.

For ~~further instructions will be sent to O.C's 124th and 151st Field Coys. R.E. regarding~~ movement orders ~~for their Companies~~ in attached table.

R.E. Park

O i/c R.E. Park will arrange with R.S.M., 34th Division to take over all books, papers, stock sheets (brought up to date) etc.

O i/c R.E. Park will arrange to return all attached men working at the Divisional Park to their respective units. R.S.M. Wright R.E. and other H.Q. ranks to return to H.Q.,R.E. ~~on morning 31st inst.~~ on evening 30th

On relief copies of all handing over documents are to be sent to this office without delay such copies to include lists in duplicate of Trench and Area Stores.

O.C. Coys. will hand over all 1/10,000, 1/20,000 and 1/40,000 maps of this area with the exception of one copy of each sheet which will be retained.

No 1/100,000 or 1/250,000 maps are to be handed over.

Signed receipts will be obtained from incoming units and copies forwarded in duplicate to this office forthwith.

Field Companies to acknowledge.

To:-
O.C. 123rd Field Coy. R.E.
O.C. 124th Field Coy. R.E.
O.C. 151st Field Coy. R.E.
O i/c R.E. Park.

29th March 1918.

D.Morgan
2nd Lieut R.E.
Assistant Adjutant, R.E.
38th Division, Royal Engineers.

TABLE TO ACCOMPANY C.R.E., 38th Division ORDER 46.

Unit.	From.	To.	Remarks.
Div. H.Q.	STEENBECK.	MERVILLE, Area.	MERVILLE.
FIELD COMPANIES R.E.			
123d Field Coy.	FORT DE NIEPPE	BOULAND Area.	Will be attached to 114th Bde. Group. MERVILLE.
124th Field Coy.	ARBITRAINES	STEENBECQUE Area	Will be attached to 115th Bde. Group. Transport by road. Personnel by lorry leaving ERQUINGHEM Church at 9 a.m. STEENBECQUE.
151st Field Coy.	L'ESTREM	"	

Entrain on Night 31st March/1st April.

V. Corps.
Third Army.

WAR DIARY

Headquarters,

ROYAL ENGINEERS, 38th Division.

A P R I L

1 9 1 8

Attached:

Operation Orders Nos. 47 to 53.

WAR DIARY
INTELLIGENCE SUMMARY
(Erase heading not required.)

Army Form C. 2118

Headquarters R.E.
38th (Welsh) Division.
April 1918
(8 sheets: sheet 1)

Vol 28

Place	Date	Hour	Summary of Events and Information	Remarks and references to Appendices
MERVILLE	31.3.18.		On 31.3.18. Moved from STEENWERCK to MERVILLE by road, with 74th Division HQ.	R.E. Op. Order No. 47 of 30/3 (3 sheets)
	1.4.18.		Left MERVILLE by Train, arrived at MONDICOURT (between DOULLENS & ARRAS) next day, moved by road to TOUTENCOURT. The C.R.E. went through by motor car on 1.4.18.	
TOUTENCOURT	2/4/18 to 12/4/18		H.Q. R.E. moved from TOUTENCOURT to CONTAY and remained at CONTAY for the rest of the month.	
CONTAY	12/4/18 to 30/4/18			
	3rd.		C.R.E. met C.E. VII Corps at ENGELBELMER and was shewn work that was to be undertaken by C.R.E. on a defensive line running from in front of ENGELBELMER southwards behind BOUZINCOURT. Work was started that night by Infantry & 115 Inf. Bde. and next day 151 Fd Co. R.E. took over the supervision of the work, with infantry. Work was continued daily till about 9th April.	
	5th.		C.R.E. met O.C. 19th Welsh Regt. (Pioneers) v.o.c.123. Th. 6. R.E. near WARLOY & started them on work on a Reserve line from near BAIZIEUX mill, towards FORCEVILLE. Work was continued daily till about 9th April. Orders were received in morning to be ready to move at 1 hours notice; these remained in force till next afternoon.	

Army Form C. 2118

WAR DIARY
INTELLIGENCE SUMMARY
(Erase heading not required.)

Place: Headquarters RE 38 (Welsh) Division.
April 1918. (2 sheets. Sheet 2.)

Date	Hour	Summary of Events and Information	Remarks and references to Appendices
7th		Capt. G.U. MORGAN, Adjt. RE. Returned from leave, having been recalled owing to military situation.	
12th		38th Div. relieved 12th Div. in line opposite ALBERT. 2 Inf. Bdes. in line: 113, 115. C.Y. R.E. placed under the orders of each (113, 123 + 151). C.R.E. worked on defensive line running in front of MILLENCOURT & in front of BOUZINCOURT, known as "Old French line", & another trench behind the "Old French line", which connected with that not had been worked on by him in front of ENGELBELMER; 124 Fd.Co. (Pioneers, with Infantry parties, carried out the work, which continued to about 28th April.	C.R.E. op. order No. 48 4/10/18 attached (1 sheet.)
25th		Part of line was to be handed over on right to 2/Australian Div. but relief was postponed for 24 hours, the entrenching then ordered again & after R.E. concerned & Pioneers had moved on 26th orders for handing over were cancelled, & they moved forward again. The relief was finally carried out on 27th, and 2 Field Coys (123 + 151) + Pioneers moved back. 124 Fd Co. & 115 Inf. Bde. remained in line, the Brig. Bde. taking over the work C.R.E. had been supervising. The above orders & counter orders are believed to have been due to enemy action at VILLERS-BRETENEUX just south of the Australians.	C.R.E. op. orders, as number attached. 51 d/23.4.18 (1 sheet) 52 d/25.4.18. (1 sheet) 53 dp6.4.8. (1 sheet)
		General. The weather during April was mostly dull & misty, with a good deal of rain during early part of month.	

T.S. Murray Wayne
CRE 38th Div.

30.4.18

OPERATION ORDERS NOS. 47 to 53.

S E C R E T   Copy No.

OPERATION ORDER No. 47
38th Divisional Royal Engineers

Ref. maps :-
    1/40,000,   30th March 1918.
    Sheets 36 and 36.A.

In continuation of my Order No. 46 addressed to 38th Division Field Coys R.E. :-

1. 38th (Welsh) Division (less Artillery) will be relieved in the Left Sector, XVth Corps, on 29th, 30th and 31st March and will be prepared to leave the XVth Corps Area by rail, entraining on the night March 31st/1st April 1918.

2. Relief of Field Coys. R.E. will be carried out in accordance with detailed table attached to my Order No. 46

3. During the period of relief command will be exercised as follows :-
   (a) G.O.C. 34th Division will take over command of the Left Sector at 10.0 a.m 31st instant.

   (b) Infantry Brigades of 34th Division located in the ERQUINGHEM Area before 10 a.m. 31st March will be under command of G.O.C. 38th Division.

   (c) While in the FTZ ACQUART Section the 170th Infantry Bde. will be under command of the G.O.C. Left Sector.

   (d) 115th Infantry Brigade will remain under the command of G.O.C. 38th Division while located in the NOUVEAU MONDE – SAILLY Area.

4. Troops will entrain from STEENBECQUE, CALONNE and MERVILLE in accordance with attached table. The average interval between trains at each Station will be three hours.

5. Entraining strengths, showing (a) Officers and other ranks.
                                 (b) Horses or mules.
                                 (c) Vehicles and number of wheels
will be handed to the R.T.O. or Officer detailed to assist at least two hours before departure of trains.

6. Units will not enter the Station precincts previous to the three hours mentioned in para. 4. Roads leading to the station will not be blocked by units, and to ensure this strict punctuality must be kept.

7. The D.A.Q.M.G., 38th Division will superintend the entrainment generally and will be at STEENBECQUE Station. Officers as under will assist him as Assistant R.T.Os.

   (a) At MERVILLE - 114th Bde.Group - 1 Officer & 1 Officer A.S.C.
   (b) At STEENBECQUE - 113th Bde Group - 1 Officer & 1 Officer A.S.C.
   (c) At CALONNE - 115th Bde Group - 1 Officer & 1 Officer A.S.C.

These Officers will report to the R.T.O. at their respective Station at least three hours before the departure of the first train, and will entrain with the last train. They are to reconnoitre at once their respective station, in order to get acquainted beforehand with the loading, etc. facilities, and the approaches to the station.

1.

8. Each Brigade Group will detail one Company and one Cooker and Team to be at their entraining station three and a half hours before departure of the first train, and report to the R.T.O. These will act as loading party for all units. They will entrain on the last train and will be under the orders of the A.S.C. Officer detailed above.

9. BILLETING.

Advance parties for billetting will be sent on in the first train from each entraining station, under Staff Captain of Brigade Groups. Two days rations will be taken.

10. Entrainment will be completed half an hour before the departure of the train.

11. Breast ropes for horse trucks must be provided by units. Ropes for vehicles will be provided by the railway.

12. All doors of covered trucks and carriages on the right hand side of the train when on the main line must be kept closed

13. ARRANGEMENTS AT DETRAINING STATION.

The D.A.A.G., 38th Division, will be in general charge at the most central station.

Staff Captains, with Billetting parties, will go by first train and will get into communication with the D.A.A.G. as early as possible.

O.C. 38th Divisional Train will detail one A.S.C. Officer for each detraining station, to go by the first train and to superintend the unloading.

Each Infantry Brigade will detail one Company, and one Cooker and Team to go in the first train and to report to R.T.O. at detraining station. The Officer in command of this Company will act as detraining Officer.

14. GENERAL INSTRUCTIONS.

Two blankets per man will be taken. All troops will move with the normal Field Service scale of transport. No extra transport will be provided, but arrangements will be made for the conveyance of extra blankets.

15. Rations. Rations to accompany troops will be :-

(a) Iron rations.
(b) Current day's rations.

In addition two days rations will be taken on trains, one in unit transport and one in supply vehicles of the Divisional Train.

All supply vehicles of the Divisional Train will move full.

16. Railhead. Railhead up to the time of entrainment will be ST. INT NOR, from whence supplies will be delivered by Horse Transport or Motor transport, according to circumstances. Refilling points will be notified later.

Railhead will be moved to the new area with effect from the second day inclusive after the day on which the first unit entrains. Until the railhead opens in the new area the portions of the supply column which have arrived there will refill from reserve supplies or other sources as may be arranged by the Army in whose area the Division will be located.

17.   Attention is drawn to 38th Division G.S.8986 reference new location of Company Headquarters to be wired immediately on occupation to 38th Division Signals.

18.   Completion of relief to be wired to this office.

19.   C.R.E's office 38th Division will close at STEENWERCK at 9 a.m. 31st inst. and will open same day at MERVILLE.

Field Companies R.E. to acknowledge.

O.C. 123rd Field Coy. R.E.
O.C. 124th Field Coy. R.E.
O.C. 151st Field Coy. R.E.

For information:-

38th Division "G"
38th Division "A" & "Q"
113th Infantry Brigade.
114th Infantry Brigade.
115th Infantry Brigade.
O.C. 19th (Welsh Regt. (Pioneers)
C.E., XVth Corps.
C.R.E., XVth Corps Troops.
C.R.E., 34th Division.
Det. 3rd Australian Tunnelling Coy.
Area Commandt. MERVILLE.
Area Commandt. STEENWERCK.
Sub-Area Commandt. ESTAIRES.

Sub-Area Commandt. NEQUINGHEM.
38th Divisional Signals.
38th Divisional Artillery.
38th Divisional Train.
C.T.O.
Assistant C.T.O.
S.S.O.
A.D.M.S.
D.A.D.O.S.
D.A.D.V.S.
War Diary.
File.

2nd Lieut. & Asst. Adjutant R.E.
38th Division, Royal Engineers.

TRAIN ARRANGEMENTS FOR MOVE OF 38TH (WELSH) DIVISION LESS ARTILLERY.

APRIL 1st. 1918

	STEENBECQUE		CAUDIQUE			MERVILLE	
No.of Train.	Time.	113th Inf.Brigade Group.	No.of Train.	Time.	115th Inf.Brigade Group.	No.of Train.	Time.	114th Inf.Brigade Group.
1.	5 am.	113th Inf.Bde.H.Q. / Bde.Signal Section. / 1 Coy.1 Cooker & Team of A.Batt / 1 Coy.M.G.Battn. / 113th T.M.Battery.	2	6.30 a.m.	115th Inf.Bde.H.Q. / Bde.Signal Section. / 1 Coy.1 Cooker & Team of A.Batt. / 1 Coy.M.G.Battn. / 115th T.M.Battery.	3	7.30 a.m.	114th Inf.Bde.H.Q. / Bde.Signal Section. / 1 Coy.1 Cooker & Team of A.Battn. / 1 Coy.M.G.Battn. / 114th T.M.Battery.
4.	8 am.	A.Battn.less 1 Coy. and Cooker.	5	9.30 a.m.	A.Battn.less 1 Coy. and Cooker.	6	10.30 a.m.	A.Battn.less 1 Coy. and Cooker.
7.	11 am	B.Battn.less 1 Coy. and Cooker.	8	12.30 p.m.	B.Battn.less 1 Coy. and Cooker.	9	1.30 p.m.	B.Battn.less 1 Coy. and Cooker.
10.	2 pm.	C.Battn.less 1 Coy. and Cooker.	11.	3.30 p.m.	C.Battn.less 1 Coy. and Cooker.	12	4.30 p.m.	C.Battn.less 1 Coy. and Cooker.
13.	5 p.m.	H.Q.,Div.Train. / 1 Coy.& Cooker B.Bn. / 124th Field Coy.RE.	14.	6.30 p.m.	19th Battn.Welsh Regt. (Pioneers).	15.	7.30 p.m.	XD.H.Q.,235 Employment Coy.,No.1 Sect.Div. Signal Coy.,H.Q.,R.E.
16.	8 pm.	H.Q.,331 Coy.A.S.C. / 151 Field Coy.R.E. / 1 Coy.& 1 Cooker C.Bn.	17	9.30 p.m.	H.Q.,333 Coy.A.S.C. / H.Q. & 1 Coy.58 Bn.MGC. / 1 Coy.& 1 Cooker B.Bn.	18	10.30 p.m.	H.Q.,332 Coy.A.S.C. / 123 Field Coy.R.E. / 1 Coy & Cooker B.Bn.
19.	11 pm.	131 Field Ambulance. / 49th Mob.Vety.Section.	20	12.30 a.m.	130th Field Ambulance / 1 Coy & Cooker C.Bn.	21	1.30 a.m.	129th Field Ambulance. / 1 Coy & Cooker C.Bn.
			22	3.30 a.m.	½ No.3 Section D.A.C.	23	4.30 a.m.	½ No.3 Section D.A.C.

X Divisional Headquarters includes Canteen, Baths, Salvage and Provost Personnel.

-3-

18. **Police Arrangements.**

The A.P.M., 38th Division will arrange for (1) the policing of the station precincts (2) a proportion of police to proceed with each Brigade Group both in the first and last trains.

H R Lee

29-3-18.

Lieutenant Colonel,
A.A. & Q.M.G., 38th (Welsh) Division.

Copies to:-

A.D.C. for G.O.C.
G.S. (3)
38th Div. Arty.
C.R.E.
38th Div. Signals
113th Bde. (2)
114th Bde. (2)
115th Bde. (2)
38th Bn., M.G.C.
19th Welsh Regt.
38th Div. Train
S.S.O.
A.D.M.S.
D.A.D.V.S.
D.A.D.O.S.
A.P.M.
38th Div. Sniping Coy.
38th Div. Gas Officer
Camp Comdt.
235th Employmt. Coy.
38th Div. HQ)
Corps R. & R. Camp)
170th Inf. Bde.

XV Corps (2)
XV Corps R.A.
D.A.D.P.S., XV Corps
57th Div.
2nd Aus. Divn.
34th Div.
Area Comdts:-
    METEREN
    FLETRE
    EEQUINGHEM
    ESTAIRES
    SAILLY
    MERVILLE
    HAVERSKERQUE
    DOULIEU
R.T.O., HAZEBROUCK
R.T.O., BOIGNY
R.T.O., MERVILLE
Div. Supervisor Posts (R.38)
A.D.R.T., PERNES
Canteen Officer, 38th Div.
Salvage Officer, 38th Div.
Baths Officer, 38th Div.

War Diary

SECRET.   Copy No. 19.

OPERATION ORDER No. 48.

38th Divisional Royal Engineers.

Map Ref. 1/40,000
Sheet 57.D.   10th April, 1918.

Information.

1. 38th Division will relieve the 12th Division in the Line about 12th instant.

2. Relief of Field Coys. R.E.

Field Coys. R.E. of 38th Division will relieve Field Coys. R.E. of 12th Division as follows :-

(a) 123rd Field Coy R.E. and attached Infantry relieves 87th Field Coy. R.E. on 11th inst. for work with left Brigade (113th Brigade)
Accommodation for personnel to be handed over, but horse lines will be retained.

(b) 151st Field Coy. R.E. and attached Infantry relieves 69th Field Coy. R.E. on 11th inst. for work with right Brigade (114th Brigade)
Accommodation for personnel to be handed over, but horse lines will be retained.

(c) Bivouac shelters will be handed over and receipts given and 151st Field Coy. R.E. will take over bivouacs shelters from 70th Field Coy. R.E. on behalf of 124th Field Coy. R.E. in addition to its own, if 70th Field Coy. R.E. moves before 124th Field Coy. R.E. arrives.

(d) 38th Division R.E's will not work on night 11/12th inst. unless special orders to do so are sent out.

(e) The party of R.E's from 123rd Field Coy. R.E. now working under orders of C.R.E., Vth Corps Troops will stop work today and rejoin their Company for work.

(f) Advance parties of 123rd and 151st Field Coys. R.E. will report at 87th and 69th Field Coys. H.Q. at 6 p.m. tonight 10th inst. and go forward tonight to see the work to be taken over.

(g) Further orders will be issued for 124th Field Coy. R.E. to move forward.

(h) 123rd and 151st Field Coys. R.E. will work under orders of Brigadiers in the line

3. Lists of all bivouacs and stores handed over and taken over will be sent to this office on completion of reliefs.

4. On completion of relief C.R.E's office and Field Coys. R.E. billets will be as follows :-

C.R.E's office   CONTAY.
123rd Field Coy. R.E., in bivouacs at V.10.b.2.7.
151st Field Coy. R.E. in bivouacs at V.10.central.
19th Pioneers.   "   "   " V.10.b.0.3.

5. Completion of reliefs to be wired to this office.

Field Coys. to acknowledge receipt.

P.T.O.

O.C. 123rd Field Coy. R.E.
O.C. 124th Field Coy. R.E.
O.C. 151st Field Coy. R.E.

For information :-

38th Division "G"	38th Divisional Signals.
38th Division "A" & "Q"	38th Divisional Train.
113th Infantry Brigade.	S.S.O.
114th Infantry Brigade.	A.D.M.S.
115th Infantry Brigade.	D.A.D.O.S.
O.C. 19th Welsh Regt. (Pioneers)	D.A.D.V.S.
C.E., Vth Corps.	War Diary.
C.R.E., Vth Corps Troops.	File.
C.R.E., 12th Division.	

Geo. W. Morgan
Captain & Adjutant, R.E.
38th Division, Royal Engineers.

SECRET   Copy No. 10.

OPERATION ORDER No. 49.

38th Divisional Royal Engineers.

18th April 1916, 10.30 a.m.

1.   119th Infantry Brigade relieves 113th Infantry Brigade in the line today and tonight.

2.   123rd Field Coy. R.E. will continue to work in the Left Brigade Area and on command being handed over from G.O.C. 113th Infantry Brigade to G.O.C. 119th Infantry Brigade, this Company will cease to be under the orders (for work) of G.O.C. 113th Infantry Brigade and come under the orders (for work) of G.O.C. 119th Infantry Brigade.

3.   No Infantry from the reserve Brigade will be available for work tonight under O.C. 124th Field Coy. R.E. or O.C. 19th Welsh Regt. (Pioneers).

4.   On the night 19/20 April only 4 Companies (not necessarily from the same Battalion) will be available for work from the reserve Brigade (115th Infantry Brigade). These will work under the directions of O.C. 19th Welsh Regt. (Pioneers) who will arrange all details direct with the Brigade, including daylight reconnaissances of the work by Officers of the Infantry working party.

5.   From the night 20/21 April inclusive onwards, two Battalions of the reserve Brigade (115th Infantry Brigade) will, as usual, be available for work on old French Line etc. One of these will work under the directions of O.C. 124th Field Coy.R.E. and the other under the directions of O.C. 19th Welsh Regt. (Pioneers) These Officers will, as usual, arrange details direct with the Brigade.

6.   As all three Brigades have had issues of picks and shovels and no more are available, no special issues of tools can be made for the above working parties.

Field Coys. to acknowledge receipt.

O.C. 123rd Field Coy. R.E.
O.C. 124th Field Coy. R.E.
O.C. 151st Field Coy. R.E.
O.C. 19th Welsh Regt. (Pioneers)

For information :-

113th Infantry Brigade.
114th Infantry Brigade.
115th Infantry Brigade.
38th Division "A"
38th Division "Q"

                                          Geo. Morgan
                                          Captain & Adjutant, R.E.
                                          38th Division Royal Engineers

War Diary

SECRET   Copy No. 6

38th Divisional Royal Engineers.

OPERATION ORDER NO. 50.

21st April 1918.

1.   113th Infantry Brigade relieves 115th Infantry Brigade in the line tonight.

2.   On relief 123rd Field Coy. R.E. will work under the orders of G.O.C. 113th Brigade and cease to be under the orders for work of G.O.C. 115th Infantry Brigade.

123rd Field Coy. R.E.
124th Field Coy. R.E.

115th Infantry Brigade.)
113th Infantry Brigade.) For information.
38th Division "G"   )

T.S. Kensall.

Lieut. Col. R.E.
C.R.E., 38th Division.

War Diary

SECRET   Copy No. 22

38th Divisional Royal Engineers.

OPERATION ORDER NO 51.

23rd April 1918.

Ref. Maps.:-
Sheet 57d.1/40,000
Sheet 62d.1/40,000

Information.

1. The 38th Division will be relieved in the line from the present Right Divisional Boundary to W.15.d.5.0. by the 2nd Australian Division on the 25th inst. and the Command will pass to the 2nd Australian Division at 6 a.m. on that date.

2. Relief of Field Companies :-

   The 123rd Field Coy. R.E. will be relieved of a portion of the left Brigade Sector from the right boundary to W.15.d.5.0. by the 2nd Australian Divisional Engineers. The remaining Northern portion of this Brigade Sector will be taken over by the 124th Field Coy. R.E. Reliefs will be completed by 6 p.m. 24th inst. O.C. 123rd Field Coy. R.E. will arrange to leave parties behind to shew parties of the 124th Field Coy. R.E. the work in the Forward Area on the night 24/25th inst. O.C. 123rd Field Coy. R.E. will get in touch with O.C. 124th Field Coy. R.E. and arrange for handing over his work.

3. 124th Field Coy. R.E. will come under the orders (for work) of G.O.C. 115th Infantry Brigade on the night 24/25th inst. and G.O.C. 115th Infantry Brigade will detail one section or more as he considers necessary for work in the forward area from the 124th Field Coy. R.E. The remainder of the Coy. will continue to work on the old French Line and the Line immediately behind (which they are now working on) under the orders of G.O.C. 115th Infantry Brigade. The 115th Infantry Brigade will supply the necessary Infantry parties for continuing the work on the old French line.
   The 124th Field Coy. R.E. billets and horse lines will remain as at present.

4. 151st Field Coy. R.E. will be relieved by the 2nd Australian Divisional Engineers on the 24th inst. The relief will be completed by 6 p.m.

5. On relief the 123rd Field Coy. R.E. will move to TOUTENCOURT and will camp at U.1.c. Arrangements are being made for tents.
   On relief 151st Field Coy. R.E. will move to TOUTENCOURT and take over the camp at U.1.c. now occupied by a Field Coy. of the 63rd Divisional Royal Engineers. An advance party should proceed tomorrow morning to take over the camp.

6. All tents will be struck and dumped at U.27.a.8.8.
   All trench shelters East of WARLOY will be handed over on relief and receipts obtained and copies sent to this office. Those shelters West of WARLOY will be dumped at U.27.a.8.8. or taken by Units to their new sites.

7. C.R.E's office will remain in CONTAY as at present.

8. Parties of Battle Surplus now employed on the Battle Headquarters under Lieut. Sampson will continue to work as at present until further orders and also the parties at present working under C.R.E. on the bath-house and horse watering points will continue to work as at present until further orders.

9. Receipts for all stores handed over will be sent to this office.

10. Completion of reliefs will be wired to this office.

Field Coys. to ac'nowledge.

Copy 1. O.C. 123rd Field Coy. R.E.
" 2. O.C. 124th Field Coy. R.E.
" 3. O.C. 151st Field Coy. R.E.

For information :-

" 4. 38th Division "G"
" 5. 38th Division "A" & "Q"
" 6. 113th Infantry Brigade.
" 7. 114th Infantry Brigade.
" 8. 115th Infantry Brigade.
" 9. O.C. 19th Welsh Regt. (Pioneers)
" 10. C.E., Vth Corps.
" 11. C.R.E., Vth Corps Troops.
" 12. C.R.E., 2nd Australian Division.
" 13. C.R.E., 35th Division.
" 14. C.R.E., 63rd Division.
" 15. 38th M.G. Battalion.
" 16. 38th Divisional Signals.
" 17. 38th Divisional Train.
" 18. S.S.O.
" 19. A.D.M.S.
" 20. D.A.D.O.S.
" 21. D.A.D.V.S.
" 22. War Diary.
" 23. File.

Captain & Adjutant R.E.
38th Division, Royal Engineers.

War Diary

SECRET.   Copy No. ....

38th Division Royal Engineers.

OPERATION ORDER NO. 52.

25th April 1918

1. The Relief of 38th Division by the 2nd Australian Division is cancelled.

2. Field Companies will move to the line today and take over work as follows :-

    123rd Field Coy. R.E. will take over all work which they handed over to the 124th Field Coy. R.E. and also all work handed over to the 2nd Australian Engineers. On completion of the relief in the line, they will come under the orders for work of the Brigadier commanding the Left Brigade.

    124th Field Coy. R.E. will hand over to the 123rd Field Coy. R.E. the work in the Forward Area which they took over from that Coy. and will take over all the work which they were previously employed on in the Old French Line and will work under the C.R.E.

    151st Field Coy. R.E. will take over all work which they handed over to the 2nd Australian Engineers and on completion of relief they will come under the orders for work of the Brigadier of the Right Brigade.

3. Field Coys. will not remove any tents from billets now occupied by them except such as they took with them. A guard will be left by each Field Coy. over all tents left behind by them until receipt of further orders. The wagon lines of Field Coys. at CONTAY will be re-occupied by them. The Battle Surplus will also remain at the wagon lines.

4. All parties of the Battle Surplus employed on Divisional Headquarters, Bath House and Horse Watering Points will continue to be so employed.

5. Reliefs will be completed by 8 p.m.
   Completion of reliefs to be wired to this office.

   Field Coys to acknowledge.

Copy 1. O.C. 123rd Field Coy. R.E.
" 2. O.C. 124th Field Coy. R.E.
" 3. O.C. 151st Field Coy. R.E.

For information :-

" 4. 38th Division "G"
" 5. 38th Division "A" & "Q"
" 6. 113th Infantry Brigade.
" 7. 114th Infantry Brigade.
" 8. 115th Infantry Brigade.
" 9. O.C. 19th Welsh Regt. (Pioneers.
" 10. C.E., Vth Corps.
" 11. C.R.E., Vth Corps Troops.
" 12. C.R.E., 2nd Australian Division.
" 13. C.R.E. 35th Division.

Copy 14. C.R.E., 63rd Division.
" 15. 38th M.G. Battalion.
" 16. 38th Div. Signals.
" 17. 38th Div. Train.
" 18. S.S.O.
" 19. A.D.M.S.
" 20. D.A.D.O.S.
" 21. D.A.D.V.S.
" 22. War Diary.
" 23. File.

Captain & Adjutant, R.E.
38th Division Royal Engineers.

War Diary

SECRET   Copy No. ....

38th Division Royal Engineers

OPERATION ORDER NO. 53.

Ref. Maps :-   26th April 1918.
Sheet 57.D. 1/40,000.
Sheet 62.D. 1/40,000.

Information.

1. The Division (less Artillery) will be relieved by troops of the 2nd Australian Division from the present right boundary to the grid line running East and West through W.15.c.5.0.

2. Command of the above part of the line will pass to G.O.C. 2nd Australian Division at 6 a.m. 27th inst. The remainder of the present Division front will remain under the command of the G.O.C., 38th Division.

Relief of Field Companies.

3. The 123rd Field Coy. R.E. will be relieved of a portion of the left Brigade Sector from the right boundary to W.15.d.5.0. by the 2nd Australian Divisional Engineers: the remaining Northern portion of this Brigade Sector will be taken over by the 124th Field Coy. R.E.
   Reliefs will be completed by 6 a.m. 27th inst.
   O.C. 123rd Field Coy. R.E. will get in touch with O.C. 124th Field Coy. R.E. and arrange for handing over his work.

4. 124th Field Coy. R.E. will cease to work under the orders of C.R.E. at 6 a.m. on 27th inst. when they will come under the orders of G.O.C. 115th Infantry Brigade for all work in the forward area and also the work on the old French line. The boundaries for work will be the new Divisional boundaries. O.C. 124th Field Coy. R.E. will detail such parties as G.O.C. 115th Infantry Brigade considers necessary for work in the forward area or the old French line.

5. 151st Field Coy. R.E. will be relieved by the 2nd Australian Divisional Engineers in the right Brigade Sector. The relief will be completed by 6 a.m. 27th inst.

6. On relief the 123rd Field Coy. R.E. will move to the camp vacated by them yesterday at TOUTENCOURT.
   On relief the 151st Field Coy. R.E. will move to the hutted camp at the Prisoners of War Cage near TOUTENCOURT vacated by them yesterday.

7. All tents will be struck and taken to the new camps. Trench shelters East of WARLOY will be handed over on relief and receipts obtained and sent to this office: those shelters West of WARLOY will be taken to the new camps.

8. Parties of the Battle Surplus now employed on various work in the back area will continue to work as at present until further orders.

9. All trench maps, photos and trench stores will be handed

over and receipts forwarded to this office. All picks and shovels issued by C.R.E. to Brigades and Field Companies will be returned to C.R.E's office CONTAY except those required for work in the new Divisional area.

10. C.R.E's office will remain at CONTAY as at present.

11. Completion of reliefs will be wired to this office.

Field Coys. to acknowledge.

Copy No. 1. O.C. 123rd Field Coy. R.E.
"   "   2. O.C. 124th Field Coy. R.E.
"   "   3. O.C. 151st Field Coy. R.E.

For information :-

"   "   4. 38th Division "G"
"   "   5. 38th Division "A" & "Q"
"   "   6. 113th Infantry Brigade.
"   "   7. 114th Infantry Brigade.
"   "   8. 115th Infantry Brigade.
"   "   9. O.C. 19th Welsh Regt. (Pioneers)
"   " 10. C.E., Vth Corps.
"   " 11. C.R.E., Vth Corps Troops.
"   " 12. C.R.E., 2nd Australian Division.
"   " 13. C.R.E., 35th Division.
"   " 14. C.R.E., 17th Division.
"   " 15. 38th M.G. Battalion.
"   " 16. Div. Signals.
"   " 17. 38th Div. Train.
"   " 18. S.S.O.
"   " 19. A.D.M.S.
"   " 20. D.A.D.O.S.
"   " 21. D.A.D.V.S.
"   " 22. War Diary.
"   " 23. File.

Captain & Adjutant, R.E.
38th Division Royal Engineers.

WAR DIARY
or
~~INTELLIGENCE SUMMARY~~
(Erase heading not required.)

Army Form C. 2118

Headquarters R.E.
38th (Welsh) Division.
May 1918 (2 sheets: sheet 1)

Vol 29

Instructions regarding War Diaries and Intelligence Summaries are contained in F.S. Regs., Part II. and the Staff Manual respectively. Title Pages will be prepared in manuscript.

Place	Date	Hour	Summary of Events and Information	Remarks and references to Appendices
CONTAY	1st		R.E. H.Q. Rvd. at CONTAY as at end of April. 124 F.Co. R.E in line with 115 Inf. Bde. near BOUZINCOURT.	C.R.E. Spooner No. 64 4/30/18
	3rd		38th Div: completed Taking over line to north of BOUZINCOURT from 35th Div: and held the line with 3 Brigades. All 3 Field Coys & Pioneer Batt'n up. Each Fd Co placed 2 Sections * either O.C or 2nd in command at disposal of Brigade as under:—	
			123 Fd Co. and 113 Inf. Bde. (Centre)	
			124 " " 115 " " (Right)	
			151 " " 114 " " (Left)	
			The remainder of each Fd Co & the Pioneer Batt'n worked under C.R.E. on PURPLE system, i.e. a line of trenches in front of BOUZINCOURT and support trenches behind it. The front trenches of this system were previously known as the "Old Trench Line". See Sheet 2 of War Diary for April 1918.	
			From 4th inst., acting on VI Corps orders, work under C.R.E was concentrated on the portion of PURPLE system immediately round BOUZINCOURT. During the month work was also done by Fd Coys under CRE, on filling in top of deep wells for a few feet (filling supported on a platform), in the case of those wells not required in front villages. BOUZINCOURT was the only village where a start was made with this work.	
			178 Tunneling Co. also worked IV Corps on Brigade Batt'n: mined dugouts, + R.A.O.P. dugouts.	
TOUTENCOURT	6th		On 6th Div. F.R.E. H.Q. moved from CONTAY to TOUTENCOURT, the front R.E.s remaining unchanged.	
			(cont.)	

WAR DIARY
INTELLIGENCE SUMMARY

Headquarters R.E.
38th (Welsh) Division.
May 1918. (2 Sheets: Sheet 2.)

Army Form C. 2118

Place	Date	Hour	Summary of Events and Information	Remarks and references to Appendices
HERISSART	20th		R.E. H.Q. moved from TOUTENCOURT to HERISSART on 35th Division taking over the line from 38th Division. Move was to have taken place next day, but was hastened by Corps Order. 124 & 6. R.E. & one company of Pioneer Battn. remained at short notice (with one inf. Battn.) under C.E. V Corps, as reserve lines of forward to work PURPLE system near SENLIS. The other two ?? Coys, & remainder of Pioneer Battn. moved out from training, the ?? Coys. going to TOUTENCOURT. Training (including musketry & several turn out & horse competitions) continued till the end of the month. R.E. H.Q. remained at HERISSART till the end of the month. With a few exceptions the weather was fine & warm throughout the month.	C.R.E. Order No. 56 4/16/18

T.S. Kennedy Lieut. Colonel.
C.R.E. 38 Div.

1/6/18

SECRET.   *War Diary*   Copy No. 22

38th Division Royal Engineers.

OPERATION ORDER NO. 54.

Ref. Map:-
Sheet 57.D. 1/40,000   30th April 1918.

Information.

1. (a) The Division (less Artillery) will relieve the 35th Division (less Artillery) in the line from W.15.a.5.6. to Q.34.d.4.0. The Command of that part of the line taken over by 115th Infantry Brigade will pass to G.O.C. 38th Division on completion of that relief on the night 1st/2nd May. The Command of the remainder of the 35th Division present front will pass to G.O.C. 38th Division on completion of relief on night 2nd/3rd May.

   (b) After relief the front will be held as a three Brigade front, 115th Infantry Brigade on the right, 113th Infantry Brigade in the centre and 114th Infantry Brigade on the left. The boundaries will be as follows :-

   Between 115th Brigade and 2nd Aust. Div. - Grid line between W.15. & 21.
   Between 115th Bde. and 113th Brigade. - E. & W. line drawn through W.9.c.central.
   Between 113th Bde. and 114th Brigade - The road at W.3.d.6.1. - W.3.central - W.2.b.central - thence along the BOUZINCOURT - MARTINSART road to the grid line between W.1. and W.7. thence due West.
   Between 114th Brigade and 17th Div. - The grid line between Squares Q and W.

Relief of Field Coys.

2. (a) The 123rd Field Coy. R.E. (now camped at Prisoners of War Cage TOUTENCOURT T.6.b.9.2.) will take over from 203 Field Coy. R.E. now in Bivouacs at V.8.a.7.7. and transport in Bivouacs at HARPENVILLE. Relief to be completed by 2 p.m. on the 1st inst.
   (b) The 124th Field Coy. R.E. (now in Bivouacs at V.8.b.2.2. and transport at U.26.c.1.0.) will remain as at present, but will extend their area for work to the left and take over from 204 Field Coy. R.E. now in Bivouacs at V.2.d.8.4.. The relief will be completed by 2 p.m. on the 2nd May.
   (c) The 151st Field Coy. R.E. now camped at Prisoners of War Cage TOUTENCOURT will take over from 205 Field Coy. R.E. now in Bivouacs at V.2.d.6.7. and transport in Bivouacs at HARPENVILLE. The relief will be completed by 2 p.m. on the 1st May.
   (d) The 19th Welsh Regt. (Pioneers) will move to the line and occupy their original bivouacs in V.3. etc., Transport to HARPENVILLE. Detailed orders have already been issued for work. Headquarters of the 35th Divisional Pioneers is North of WARLOY-HEDAUVILLE Road. 19th Welsh Regt. (Pioneers) will take over from the 35th Divisional Pioneers all maps, trench stores etc.

3. (a) Each Field Coy. will place two sections under the command for work of Brigadiers as under and either the O.C. or his 2nd in command will also be under the orders for work of the Brigadier:-
   124th Field Coy. R.E. with 115th Infantry Brigade.
   123rd Field Coy. R.E. with 113th Infantry Brigade.
   151st Field Coy. R.E. with 114th Infantry Brigade.

1.

(b) At 2 p.m. 2nd May the 124th Field Coy. R.E. (less the two Sections detailed in para. 3 (a) above) will cease to work under the orders of the Brigadier 115th Infantry Brigade, and all Field Coys. and Pioneers will come under the orders for work of C.R.E., 38th Division at 2 p.m. 2nd May; The two Sections detailed to Brigadiers in para 3 (a) above will come under the orders of Brigadiers when the Brigadiers concerned take over command of their respective Brigade Sectors.

(c) The remainder of each Field Coy. and the Pioneers will work directly under C.R.E. on the ENGLEBELMER - MILLENCOURT line. Orders (with tracings shewing the portions of the line allotted) to each of the above units and Pioneers for work purposes, have already been issued to units concerned. Each Field Coy. will have for work every 24 hours half a Battalion from the reserve Battalion of its Brigade: arrangements to be made direct between each Field Coy. and its Brigade. Work will commence as soon as possible after Field Coys. and Pioneers move in, and arrangements will be made in advance to ensure that the half Battalion is employed in each case as soon as it is available.

(d) The Bivouac accommodation the 123rd Field Coy. R.E. and the 151st Field Coy. R.E. will take over from the 203rd Field Coy. R.E. and the 205th Field Coy. R.E. respectively in the line may not be sufficient to accommodate the attached Infantry and the Bivouac accommodation the 124th Field Coy. R.E. will take over from the 204th Field Coy. R.E. will be available to make up the extra accommodation required. The 123rd Field Coy. R.E. and the 151st Field Coy. R.E. will hand over all tents and shelters now on their charge to their relieving Coys. and they will take over all tents and trench shelters from their opposite numbers at their forward bivouacs and horse lines.

R.E. Stores.

4. The following will be the arrangements for the supply of R.E. stores :-

(a) Staff Captains of Brigades will indent direct upon C.R.E. for stores required by Brigades for work in the Brigade area after consultation with the R.E. attached to them.

(b) R.E's and Pioneers working on the ENGLEBELMER - MILLENCOURT line will indent direct on the C.R.E..

(c) It will greatly facilitate the issue of stores if all indents are submitted the day previous to that on which they are required to be drawn.

5. Wiring is to be considered as of the first importance and to enable me to meet the demands for wire and pickets, units should not have more than one day's supply on the job, otherwise the hoarding by one unit of stocks will hold up the work of other units.

6. Special care must be taken of all picks and shovels and when they are not required they should be returned to the Divisional R.E. Dump. Up to the present moment over 2,000 shovels issued by C.R.E. are still in the possession of units and the difficulty of obtaining further supplies has already been pointed out to units.

7. All details of relief will be arranged between Units direct.

8.   All trench maps, air photos, trench stores and demolition schemes will be taken over and lists forwarded to this office by 1st D.R. on the 3rd inst. Field Coys. will report by wire immediately on completion of relief whether all demolition schemes are complete in every detail or otherwise. Copies of all demolition schemes held and taken over will be sent to this office by last D.R. on the 3rd inst.

9.   C.R.E's headquarters will remain at CONTAY.

10. Completion of reliefs will be wired to this office.

Field Coys. to acknowledge.

```
Copy No. 1.   O.C. 123rd Field Coy. R.E.
   "    "  2.   O.C. 124th Field Coy. R.E.
   "    "  3.   O.C. 151st Field Coy. R.E.

              For information :-

   "    "  4.   38th Division "G"
   "    "  5.   38th Division "A" & "Q"
   "    "  6.   113th Infantry Brigade.
   "    "  7.   114th Infantry Brigade.
   "    "  8.   115th Infantry Brigade.
   "    "  9.   O.C. 19th Welsh Regt. (Pioneers)
   "    " 10.   C.E. Vth Corps.
   "    " 11.   C.R.E. Vth Corps Troops.
   "    " 12.   C.R.E., 2nd Australian Division.
   "    " 13.   C.R.E. 35th Division.
   "    " 14.   C.R.E. 17th Division.
   "    " 15.   38th M.G. Battalion.
   "    " 16.   38th Div Signals.
   "    " 17.   38th Div. Train.
   "    " 18.   S.S.O.
   "    " 19.   A.D.M.S.
   "    " 20.   D.A.D.O.S.
   "    " 21.   D.A.D.V.S.
   "    " 22.   War Diary.
   "    " 23.        File.
```

signature: Morgan
Captain & Adjutant R.E.
38th Division Royal Engineers.

War Diary

Copy No. 20

38th Division, Royal Engineers.

OPERATION ORDER NO. 56.

16th May 1918.

Ref. Map :-
Sheet 57.D.1/40,000

1. INFORMATION.

    (a) 38th Division (less Artillery) will be relieved by 35th Division (less Artillery) in the AVELUY Sector of the Vth Corps Front.

    (b) The Command of the Sector will pass to the General Officer Commanding 35th Division at 10. a.m. 21st inst. at which hour 38th Division Headquarters will close at TOUTENCOURT and open at HERISSART.

2. RELIEF OF FIELD COMPANIES.

    (a)   123rd Field Coy. R.E. will be relieved as follows :-

    205th Field Coy. R.E. will take over the bivouacs in V.5.a. and transport lines near HARPONVILLE; also the work of the two Sections attached to the Centre Brigade and the work on the PURPLE System under C.R.E..
    On completion of relief 123rd Field Coy. R.E. and transport will move to TOUTENCOURT and take over camp at Prisoners' of War Cage now occupied by 205th Field Coy. R.E.

    (b)   124th Field Coy. R.E. will be relieved as follows, but will remain as at present, in bivouacs at V.8,b.2.8. and transport lines at HARPONVILLE :-

    204th Field Coy. R.E. will take over the work of the two Sections attached to Right Brigade and also the work on the PURPLE System under C.R.E.
    On completion of relief the 124th Field Coy. R.E. will come under the orders of Chief Engineer, Vth Corps for work.

    (c)   151st Field Coy. R.E. will be relieved as follows :-

    203rd Field Coy. R.E. will take over the work on PURPLE System under C.R.E. and the work of the two Sections attached to the Left Brigade, also bivouacs at V.5.a. and transport lines at HARPONVILLE.
    On completion of relief 151st Field Coy. R.E. and transport will move to TOUTENCOURT and take over camp at Prisoners' of War Cage now occupied by 203rd Field Coy. R.E.

    (d)   Reliefs of Field Coys. will be completed by 2 p.m. 20th inst.

3.   123rd and 151st Field Coys. R.E. will hand over all trench shelters forward of their transport lines but will not hand over trench shelters and tents at their wagon lines.

4.   All trench maps, air photos, trench stores (except in the case of 124th Field Coy. R.E.) demolition schemes and defence schemes, also all work in hand or proposed, will be handed over and lists forwarded to this office by first D.R. on 22nd inst.

(5)   C.R.E's Headquarters will close at TOUTENCOURT at 10 a.m. 21st inst. and move to HERISSART.

(6)   Completion of reliefs will be wired to this office.

(7)   Field Coys. to acknowledge.

Copy No. 1.   O.C. 123rd Field Coy. R.E.
"   "   2.   O.C. 124th Field Coy. R.E.
"   "   3.   O.C. 151st Field Coy. R.E.

For information :-

Copy No. 4.   38th Division "G"
"   "   5.   38th Division "A" & "Q"
"   "   6.   113th Infantry Brigade.
"   "   7.   114th Infantry Brigade.
"   "   8.   115th Infantry Brigade.
"   "   9.   O.C. 19th Welsh Regt. (Pioneers).
"   " 10.   C.E. Vth Corps.
"   " 11.   C.R.E., 35th Division.
"   " 12.   C.R.E., Vth Corps Troops.
"   " 13.   38th M.G. Battalion.
"   " 14.   38th Div. Signals.
"   " 15.   38th Div. Train.
"   " 16.   S.S.O.
"   " 17.   A.D.M.S.
"   " 18.   D.A.D.O.S.
"   " 19.   D.A.D.V.S.
"   " 20.   War Diary.
"   " 21.   File.

Captain & Adjutant, R.E.
38th Division Royal Engineers.

War Diary.

Note :- This paper cancels that issued 18th May 1918.

183rd Field Coy. R.E. and 181st Field Coy. R.E.

TRAINING COMPETITIONS.

1. The following competitions for which prizes will be awarded will be held by 183rd and 181st Field Coys. in (say) about a weeks time :-

   A. **MUSKETRY.** Inter-Section falling tile competition. (Dismounted N.C.O's and men)

   B. **MUSKETRY.** Inter-Section rapid fire competition. (Dismounted N.C.O's and men)

   C. **MUSKETRY.** Inter-Company rapid fire competition (Mounted men).

   D. **GENERAL TURNOUT.** Inter-Section, for R.E.

   E. **DRAUGHT HORSES.** harness and Drivers. Inter-Company.

   F. **Riding Horses, harness and Riders.** Inter-Company.

2. To provide ammunition for competitions A, B and C, each Field Company will reserve 950 rounds from its allotment.

3. These competitions are intended to be an encouragement to all ranks in training, and have been framed with a view to the points needing special attention.

4. Details of competitions are as under :-
   A. One section from each Company. These will be selected by Company Commanders by means of a preliminary competition, conducted on the same lines as a final competition.
   Each Section will consist of 25 (N.C.O's and men, R.E.) To be divided into 5 parties of 5 each.
   Range : 30 yards.
   Rounds : 10 per man.
   Time limit : 1 minute.
   Targets : tiles, bottles or other suitable targets about 4" x 4" one per man.
   Prize : 5 francs per man of winning section.
   Method of conducting. The first party of five from each section will be prone. Rifles unloaded and at safety, magazine empty; cut off open; two clips on the ground.
   On the order to commence, independent fire will be opened. For every target knocked down by party, the corresponding member of the other party to be put out of action. Fire to cease when all the targets of one party have been knocked down, or at the expiration of one minute. Any unfired rounds to be forfeited. One mark to be awarded to each party for every target that the other party has failed to knock down.

A, B & C were held 30.5.18.   P.T.O.
E & F
D was held 1.6.18.

The second and subsequent parties of five from each Section to compete in the same manner.
The marks gained by each of the five parties of a Section to be added together, and the Section with the highest total to win.

B. One Section from each Company.
These will be selected by Company Commanders by means of a preliminary competition, conducted on the same lines as the final competition. Each Section will consist of 25 (N.C.O's and men R.E.) to be divided into five parties of five each.

 Range: 30 yards.
 Rounds: 10 per man.
 Time limit: 30 seconds.
 Targets: 2 small figure targets or other suitable targets for each party of five.
 Prize: 5 francs per man of winning section.
 Method of conducting: The first party of five from each Section will be prone, one round in chamber, rifle at safety, left forearm on ground, 4 rounds in magazine, cut off open. On the order to commence, rapid fire will be opened. Fire to cease at the expiration of 30 seconds from the order to commence. Any unfired rounds to be forfeited. Each party will score one mark for every hit on its target. Ricochets not to count as hits.
 The second and subsequent parties of five from each section to compete in the same manner. The marks gained by each of the five parties of a section to be added together and the section with the highest total to win.

C. All details the same as B, except that each Company will furnish one team of 30 selected without preliminary competition from its mounted N.C.O's, Drivers and Batmen.

D. Each Company will parade as strong as possible with vehicles, in 4 sections and Headquarters.

 Dress :- Marching Order.

 Vehicles :- Each Section: 1 double tool cart.
 (Horsed)   1 double limber.
            1 pack animal.
      Headquarters: 3 Pontoon wagons.
            1 G.S. wagon.
            1 water cart.
            1 cook's cart.
            Spare horses.
 Tool carts and limbers to be equipped with tools etc. but no baggage to be loaded.
 Pontoon wagons to be as issued (i.e. no temporary superstructure)
 Pack animals equipped.

Marks will be awarded for general smartness, cleanness and condition of Officers, N.C.O's and men, vehicles, equipment, horses, harness, clothing etc. etc. Marks will not be deducted for shabbiness due to fair wear and tear. Metal parts of vehicles which are unpainted to be polished.

Sections and Headquarters (including mounted parts in both cases) will called upon to carry out simple movements including saluting, and the way these are done will be taken into account in marking.

A prize of 200 francs will be given to the best section. In deciding which is the best section, account will be taken of the Headquarters of the Company to which it belongs. For this purpose, one third of the total marks will be allotted for the Headquarters, and two thirds for the section. The award will be based on the total marks gained.

A prize of 100 francs will be given to the Headquarters gaining highest marks.

E. A prize of 10 francs to the Driver of the best pair of draught horses with harness. Turnout of Driver will be taken into account in marking.
5 entries per Company.

F. A prize of 10 francs to the rider (N.C.O.) of the best riding horse, with saddlery. Turnout of rider (who will be mounted) will be taken into account in marking.
5 entries per Company.

5. In musketry competitions, no allowance will be made for jambs or miss fires. If ties occur, the C.R.E. will arrange at the time how they are to be decided.

6. Abstract of Prizes :-

	Francs.
A.	125.
B.	125.
C.	~~225.~~ 200
D.	300.
E.	10.
F.	10.
Total.	~~705.~~ 770

Divisional Headquarters is granting funds to cover this.

24th May 1918.

Geo. A. Brogue
Captain, R.E.
for Lieut. Col. R.E.
C.R.E., 38th Division.

SECRET.

ORIGINAL   WAR   DIARY   -   June   1918

-:-:-:-:-:-:-:-:-:-:-:-:-:-:-:-

Headquarters, 38th Divisional Royal Engineers.

* * * * * * * *

1. 7. 1918.

Army Form C. 2118

WAR DIARY
or
INTELLIGENCE SUMMARY

Headquarters R.E.
38th (Welsh) Division.

JUNE 1918   (Sheets – ONE)

(Erase heading not required.)

Instructions regarding War Diaries and Intelligence Summaries are contained in F.S. Regs., Part II. and the Staff Manual respectively. Title Pages will be prepared in manuscript.

Place	Date	Hour	Summary of Events and Information	Remarks and references to Appendices
HERRISART	1		R.E. H.Qrs. at Herrisart. Inspection of 124th and 151st Field Coys.R.E. by C.R.E. in connection with General Turn Out Competition.	
	5		38th Division relieves the 63rd (R.N) Division in the MESNIL Sector. Field Companies relieved as under :-	
			123rd Field Co. took over from 247th Field Co.R.E.	
			124th do. do. 249th do. do.	
			151st do. do. 248th do. do.	
LEALVILLERS	6		C.R.E. H.Qrs. moved to LEALVILLERS.	
			Details of relief completed by 2 a.m. on 6th June Disposition of each Field Company R.E. as follows:- Two Sections from each Company working under C.R.E. on The Intermediate System, Deep Dugouts and Wiring. 1 Section each from 123rd and 124th Field Coys. attached for work to Left and Right Brigades respectively.	
			1 Section 151st Field Co. employed on Demolition preparations in Divisional Area.	
			1 Section each Company in Rest at Transport Lines. Employed on tracks and back area work generally.	
	21		Lieut.Col.Kelsall, D.S.O.,R.E., admitted to Hospital sick and evacuated to C.C.S.	
	24		Received warning note that Division would probably be relieved by 35th Division on the 2nd and 3rd July, relief to be completed by 4th.	
	28		Notified that relief was postponed probably for a fortnight.	
	29		Lieut.Col. D.Grant Dalton, D.S.O., Comdg. 19th Welsh Regt. assumes Acting C.R.E.	
			GENERAL - Weather during first week very fine, later cooler and dull with some rain, and very fine towards end of month. A peculiar kind of Influenza prevalent amongst R.E's during last 2 weeks.	

1-7-18

Grant Dalton L^t.152
C.R.E. 38th (Welsh) Division.

War Diary

S E C R E T.   Copy No. ....

38th Division, Royal Engineers.

OPERATION ORDER NO. 59.

--------oOo--------

Ref. Map :-
Sheet 57.D.1/40,000   1st June, 1918.

1. INFORMATION.

    (a)   38th Division (less Artillery) will relieve 63rd Division (less Artillery) in the MESNIL Sector.

    (b)   The Command of the Divisional Sector will pass on completion of the relief of the whole Division on the night 5/6th June.

    (c)   The 124th Field Coy. R.E., the Battalion of the 114th Infantry Brigade and the Company of the 19th Battalion Welsh Regt. (Glamorgan Pioneers) will cease work under the Chief Engineer, Vth Corps, after the 2nd June 1918.

2. RELIEF OF FIELD COMPANIES

    (a)   Field Companies R.E. of the 38th Division will relieve Field Companies R.E. of the 63rd Division as laid down in the attached Table of Reliefs.

    (b)   Reliefs will be completed by 2 a.m. on the 6th June 1918, but Field Companies will arrange to take over all demolition schemes by 8 p.m. on the 5th June and after that hour will arrange to supply the necessary parties for the sitting charges.

    (c)   The 63rd Division Defence Scheme will be taken over and acted on until further orders. O.C's Field Companies will ensure that all Officers and N.C.O's are thoroughly acquainted with this scheme before the relief is completed.

3.   All movement EAST of the ACHEUX - VARENNES Road will be made under cover of darkness and by sections at 200 yards interval.

4.   Advance parties of 1 Officer and 8 O.R. from each Field Coy. will report to the transport lines of their opposite numbers at 2 p.m. on the 4th June and will be guided to their forward billets under Company arrangements on the night 4/5th June. In addition, O.C's Field Companies will arrange to get in touch with their opposite numbers and send the necessary parties to go over the work.

5.   Each Field Company will place one section under the

command for work of Brigadiers as under :-

    123rd Field Coy. R.E. with the 113th Infantry Brigade.
    124th Field Coy. R.E. with the 114th Infantry Brigade.
    151st Field Coy. R.E. with the 115th Infantry Brigade.

6.   (a) All trench maps, photographs, ammunition and trench and billet stores will be taken over and list of same forwarded to this office.

    (b) The following list of tents and shelters will be taken over on relief. Any deficiencies in taking over will be immediately reported to this office :-

Shelters.

    247th Field Coy. (by 123rd Field Coy.) FORCEVILLE.   5.
    248th Field Coy. (by 151st Field Coy.) P.36.b.9.2.   9.
    249th Field Coy. (by 124th Field Coy.) HEDAUVILLE. 10.

                                          Total - 24

7.   The camps now occupied by 38th Division R.E. will be taken over by 63rd Division R.E. as follows :-

    249th Field Coy. will take over from 123rd Field Coy.
    247th Field Coy. will take over from 124th Field Coy.
    248th Field Coy. will take over from 151st Field Coy.

    Field Coys will hand over all orders and maps concerning the action of the Right Supporting Division, and all information as to training grounds and ranges to their opposite numbers. All target material and range appliances will be handed over.

8.   Copies of all demolition schemes will be taken over and a report is to be sent in to this office by first D.R. on the 8th inst. whether same are complete or otherwise.

9.   <u>R.E. STORES.</u>

    Divisional R.E. Park will be situated at O.23.d. All indents for R.E. material must reach C.R.E. office by 4 p.m. daily the day previous to that on which they are required to be drawn.
    Divisional R.E. Park will be closed for all issues at 8 p.m. daily.

10.   C.R.E. Headquarters will close at HERRISSART at 7 p.m. 5th June and will move to LEALVILLERS.

11.   Completion of reliefs to be wired to this office.

12.   Field Companies to acknowledge.

Copy No.			Copy No.		
" "	1.	123rd Field Coy. R.E.	" "	13.	C.R.E., 35th Div.
" "	2.	124th Field Coy. R.E.	" "	14.	C.R.E. 63rd Div.
" "	3.	151st Field Coy. R.E.	" "	15.	38th M.G. Battn.
		For information :-	" "	16.	38th Div. Sigs.
" "	4.	38th Div. "G"	" "	17.	38th Div. Train.
" "	5.	38th Div. "A & Q"	" "	18.	S.S.O.
" "	6.	113th Bde.	" "	19.	A.D.M.S.
" "	7.	114th Bde.	" "	20.	D.A.D.O.S.
" "	8.	115th Bde.	" "	21.	D.A.D.V.S.
" "	9.	19th Welsh Regt	" "	22.	War Diary.
" "	10.	C.E., V Corps.	" "	23.	File.
" "	11.	C.R.E., 12th Div.	" "	24.	File.
" "	12.	C.R.E., 17th Div.			

                                                            Captain & Adjutant R.E
                                                            38th Division Royal Engineers

TABLE OF FIELD COMPANY RELIEFS
to accompany
C.R.E., 38th Division, Operation Order No.59.

---oOo---

Serl. No.	Date. June.	Unit.	From	Tp.	Unit.	Transport Lines.	Brigade Sector.	Remarks.
1.	5/6	123rd Fd Coy.	TOUTENCOURT	PURPLE LINE Q.19.a.9.4.	247 Fd Coy.	CLAIRFAYE O.30.a.	Left (113 Brigade)	Transport and reserve Sec. will move on morning 6th June.
2.	5/6	124th Fd Coy.	R.E. Bivouacs at V.8. and transport Lines at U.16.	PURPLE LINE P.36.b.9.2.	249 Fd Coy.	CLAIRFAYE O.30.a.	Right (114 Brigade)	124 Fd Coy. will be relieved by 247 Fd Coy. Transport & reserve Sec. will move on morning 6 June.
3.	5/6	151 Fd Coy.	TOUTENCOURT.	PURPLE LINE P.30.d.9.3.	248 Fd Coy.	CLAIRFAYE O.30.a.	Centre (115 Brigade)	Transport and reserve Seq will move on morning 6 June.
4.	5th	C.R.E. 38 Div.	HERISSART.	LEALVILLERS O.23.b.1.4.	G.R.E. 63 Div.	O.23.b.1.4.		

War Diary

SECRET.   Copy No. 8

38th Division, Royal Engineers.

OPERATION ORDER NO. 60.

Ref. Map :-
Sheet 57.D.1/40,000.   6th June 1918.

1. INFORMATION.

   (a) The Divisional Sector (MESNIL Sector) now held as a three *B'de front* will in future be held by two Brigades in the line and one in reserve, and the following reliefs will be completed by 5 a.m. 7th inst :-

   (b)   The 115th Infantry Brigade will relieve the 114th Infantry Brigade (less the reserve Battalion).

   (c)   The 113th Infantry Brigade will relieve the troops of 115th Infantry Brigade (less the reserve Battalion and less the Company in Q.26.a.) as far South as the following boundary :-
   DRAKE ALLEY - JAMES AVENUE - GRASS AVENUE as far as Q.27. central, and thence along the grid line due West.
   The above will constitute the boundary between the two Brigades; the communication trenches mentioned will be common to both.

   (d)   114th Infantry Brigade (less Headquarters) on relief will withdraw to bivouacs hitherto occupied by the reserve Battalions at P.27.b.3.3., P.27.b.8.3. and P.22.a.7.3., and will relieve the Companies of 113th and 115th Infantry Brigades in the PURPLE LINE. 114th Infantry Brigade Headquarters will remain at P.32.a.1.8. H.Q. of the 114th L.T.M.Battery may remain at their present location if desired.

   (e)   The present dispositions by Companies will be maintained until further orders, and Brigadier Generals Commanding Brigades in the line are responsible for the defence of the PURPLE LINE within their boundaries, and will take command of troops in that line in accordance with 63rd Division Defence Scheme.

   (f)   The Battalion H.Q. at Q.28.a.9.5. will belong to 115th Infantry Brigade for the present.

2.   The following readjustments will be made by Field Companies R.E. :-

   (i)   The Section of the 123rd Field Coy. R.E. attached to the 113th Infantry Brigade for work forward will, in addition to the work in the present Brigade area, take over all work from the Section of the 151st Field Coy. R.E. as far South as the new Right boundary of the Left Brigade.

(ii) The Section of the 124th Field Coy. R.E. at present attached to the 114th Infantry Brigade for work forward will, in addition to the work in the present Brigade Area, take over from the Section of the 151st Field Coy. R.E. all work as far North as the now Left Boundary of the Right Brigade and will come under the orders of the Brigadier of the 115th Infantry Brigade on completion of the Brigade relief.

(iii) The Section of the 151st Field Coy. R.E. attached to the 115th Infantry Brigade for work forward will, on completion of the Brigade reliefs, rejoin the 151st Field Coy. R.E. and come under the orders of the C.R.E. for work.

3. O.C's Sections of the 123rd Field Coy. R.E. and 124th Field Coy. R.E. attached to Brigades for work forward will get in touch with O.C. Section 151st Field Coy. R.E. attached to the 115th Infantry Brigade as soon as possible, and arrange for taking over the work.

4. Completion of reliefs to be wired to this office.

5. Field Companies R.E. to acknowledge.

```
Copy No. 1.  123rd Field Coy. R.E.
  "   "  2.  124th Field Coy. R.E.
  "   "  3.  151st Field Coy. R.E.

            For information :-

  "   "  4.  38th Division "G"
  "   "  5.  113th Infantry Brigade.
  "   "  6.  114th Infantry Brigade.
  "   "  7.  115th Infantry Brigade.
  "   "  8.  War Diary.
  "   "  9.  File.
  "   " 10.   "
```

Lieut. R.E. for
Captain & Adjutant R.E.
38th Division, Royal Engineers.

SECRET.   Copy No. 8

                    38th Division, Royal Engineers.

                    OPERATION ORDER NO 61.

                                              30th June 1916.

1.   115th Brigade will relieve 113th Brigade in the Left Sub-Sector on the night 22nd/23rd June.

2.   The Section of the 123rd Field Coy. R.E. attached to the 113th Brigade for work will, on completion of the relief, come under the orders for work of the G.O.C. 115th Infantry Brigade.

3.   Field Coys. R.E. to acknowledge.

Copy No. 1. O.C. 123rd Field Coy. R.E.
  "   " 2. O.C. 124th Field Coy. R.E.
  "   " 3. O.C. 151st Field Coy. R.E.

           For information :-

  "   " 4. 38th Division "A"
  "   " 5. 113th Infantry Brigade.
  "   " 6. 114th Infantry Brigade.
  "   " 7. 115th Infantry Brigade.
  "   " 8. War Diary.
  "   " 9. File.

                                        G'rout Morgan
                                        Captain & Adjutant R.E.
                                        38th Division Royal Engineers.

Army Form C. 2118

WAR DIARY
or
INTELLIGENCE SUMMARY
(Erase heading not required.)

Headquarters, 38th Division
Royal Engineers.

July 1918.

Instructions regarding War Diaries and Intelligence Summaries are contained in F.S. Regs., Part II. and the Staff Manual respectively. Title Pages will be prepared in manuscript.

WO 31

Place	Date	Hour	Summary of Events and Information	Remarks and references to Appendices
LEAIVILLERS.	10th		Major Wood Acting C.R.E., took over from Lieut. Col. D.Grant Dalton,	
	15.	11 a.m.	Conference G.S.O.1 and C.R.E. 21st Division reference relief: at 38th Div. "G" office.	
	16.		Conference C.R.E's 63rd and 17th Divisions reference relief: at C.R.E. 38th Div. Office.	
	17.	9.30 a.m.	Visit from Chief Engineer, re work on BROWN LINE and Pill Boxes for 17th Division.	
	18.		123rd and 124th Field Coys. to TOUTENCOURT for training.	
	19.		Visit BROWN LINE with O.C. 151st Field Coy. R.E. and Adjutant.	
	20.		151st Field Coy. R.E. start work on BROWN LINE and Pill Boxes for 17th Division & Battalion of 113 Bde.	
TOUTENCOURT.	26		123rd Field Coy. R.E. preparing jumps for Divisional Horse Show.	
	27		Divisional R.E. Sports)(partly postponed.) Owing to rain and mud.	
	28		Horse Show.)postponed.	
	29		Move C.R.E's Office from LEAIVILLERS to TOUTENCOURT.	
	31		Visit Divisional Reception Camp VALHEUREUX with Adjutant reference work on Baths and Cookhouses also AUXI-le-CHATEAU re purchase of lime.	

2/8/1918.

[signature]
Major R.E.
A/C.R.E., 38th Division.

CRE
38th Div
Aug. 1918

WAR DIARY
INTELLIGENCE SUMMARY

Headquarters,
Royal Engineers, 38th Division.

August 1918. (sheets. Sheet 1.)

Army Form C. 2118

Vol 32

Place	Date	Hour	Summary of Events and Information	Remarks and references to Appendices
TOUTENCOURT	1 – 5th		Moved to shelters in gully at 0.22.d.2.7.	
Near LEAL-VILLERS	5th		Lieut. Col. T.E.Kedsall R.E. resumed the appointment of C.R.E.,38th Division on return from sick leave. Major J.C.I. Wood, O.O. 123rd Field Coy. R.E. who had been acting as C.R.E. since 10/7/18 with the acting rank of Lieut. Col. ceased to hold that rank after 5th August. Up to about the middle of the month work was continued on concrete M.G.Pill Boxes and the preparation of selected trenches for winter use. About the 8th, however, R.E. reconnaissances of crossings of the River ANCRE were started, with a view to being prepared to follow up the enemy if he retired.	
	24th 8th			
	13th- 19th		Lieut. Col. Kelsall R.E. acted for Brig.General Stevenson as C.E. Vth Corps, while the latter was on leave.	
	20th		C.R.E. held a conference with Os.-C. Field Coys. and Divisional Pioneers (19th Welsh Regt.) regarding action in case of enemy retirement.	
	23rd		As a result of a Corps Commander's conference at 10. a.m. C.R.E. visited all three Infantry Brigade H.Qrs. with reference to ANCRE Crossings and at 4 p.m. had a conference with Os.C 123rd and 151st Field Coys. and O.C. Pioneers. At this latter conference the action to be taken by R.E. and Pioneers in connection with the attack by 38th Division on night 23rd/24th Augt. was explained as recorded in C.R.E's Operation Order No. 67 dated 23/8/18. 151st Field Coy. R.E. continued working on the Bridge mentioned in para. 7 (a) of Operation Order No. 67 and 123rd Field Coy. R.E. continued working on bridge mentioned in para.5 (c) of Operation Order No. 67. Assistance was given by Divisional Pioneers and labour units as available and required Approaches were improved and bridges strengthened and improved.	C.R.E's Op.Order No.67 d/ 23/8/18 (1sheet) & notes on same (1 sheet) attached

Army Form C. 2118

Headquarters,
Royal Engineers, 38th Divz
Sheet 2.

WAR DIARY (Continued)
or
INTELLIGENCE SUMMARY
(Erase heading not required.)

Instructions regarding War Diaries and Intelligence Summaries are contained in F.S. Regs., Part II. and the Staff Manual respectively. Title Pages will be prepared in manuscript.

Place	Date	Hour	Summary of Events and Information	Remarks and references to Appendices
Near HEDAU-VILLE	24th		R.E.,H.Qrs. moved from near LEALVILLERS to Dugouts in the road bank at V.3.B.8.2.	
USNA REDOUBT.	26th 28th 28th		R.E.,H.Qrs. moved from near HEDAUVILLE to tents at USNA REDOUBT (W.24.b.3.7.) Pioneers withdrawn from work under C.R.E. to be placed in Divisional Reserve. Pioneers and 124th Field Coy. R.E. placed under orders of C.R.E. for digging a defensive line from East Corner of HIGH WOOD to a point West of LONGUEVAL. Order was received by C.R.E.,6 p.m and parties were collected and distributed on the work by morning 28th/29th a series of small posts (15 in number) being dug. The posts were mostly improvements of old trenches and shell holes of the 1916 battles. Owing to advance by Division on 29th nothing further was done to improve this defensive line.	C.R.E. Op. Order No.68.
	30th) 31st)		**Pioneers and 3 Field Coys. employed under C.R.E. on roads and bridges over R.ANCRE.**	
			During the first part of the month a Company of 305th U.S.Engineers was attached to C.R.E.,38th Division for instruction. Two different Coys. were so attached in succession.	

Lieut. Col. R.E.
C.R.E.,38th Division.
August 1918.

Army Form C. 2123.
(In books of 100.)

MESSAGES AND SIGNALS.

No. of Message..............

| Prefix.... Code.... Words 16 | Received From YC1A By ..... | Sent, or sent out. At..........m. To .... By .... | Office Stamp. YC11A 26/9/18 |

Charges to Collect
Service Instructions.   y H

Handed in at...... Office...... m. Received ...... m.

TO   38 Div G

*Sender's Number	Day of Month	In reply to Number	A A A
E 121	26		
Bridge	depot	down	
	change		

G.S.O. 1
G.S.O. 2
G.S.O. 3
G.S.O. 4

FROM   C R E
TIME & PLACE

*This line should be erased if not required

MESSAGES AND SIGNALS.

TO

6-57 am.

"A" Form.
MESSAGES AND SIGNALS.
Army Form C. 2121.
(In pads of 100.)

TO	38th Division, G.S.	
Sender's Number.	Day of Month.	In reply to Number.	AAA
* R.E. 3861	16		AAA

In confirmation of telephone message sent you this morning AAA
151 Field Coy R.E. report Crossing effected midnight last night along Causeway eastward from Q.36.c.6.7. AAA

[Stamp: GENERAL STAFF 38th (WELSH) DIVISION 16/8/18]

GSS/18

G.S.O. 1	
G.S.O. 2	
G.S.O. 3	
G.S.O. 4	

12·6 pm.

From C.R.E., 38th Divn.
Place
Time

(Z) Lt. R.E.

War Diary.

SECRET.　　　　　　　　　　　　　　　Copy No. 16

38th Division Royal Engineers

C.R.E's Operation Order No. 67.

23rd August, 1918.

1. The 38th Division together with other troops on both flanks will attack the enemy positions east of the River ANCRE on the night 23/24th August, 1918.
   Further particulars and the orders in paras 4 – 10, were communicated verbally to officers Commanding 123 and 151 Field Coys R.E. and O.C. 19th Welsh Regt. (Pioneers) at C.R.E's Conference today.

2. The duties allotted to Field Companies and Pioneers are as under:-

3. 124 Field Coy R.E. has already been detailed as follows :-

    (a) Company, less 2 sections, placed under orders of G.O.C. 113 Infantry Brigade.

    (b) 1 section under orders of G.O.C. 114 Infantry Brigade.

    (c) 1 section under orders of G.O.C. 115 Infantry Brigade.

4. The remaining 2 Field Coys and Divisional Pioneers will work under the orders of the C.R.E. and carry out the following tasks.

5. 123 Field Coy R.E. will

    (a) make crossings of the ANCRE fit for Infantry in single file at :
    Q.29.b.8.0.
    Q.24.c.5.0.
    It is essential that this work be put in hand immediately it is dark enough and completed as soon as possible.
    (b) Make the road from MESNIL through Q.29.a and b to Q.24.a.1.5. sufficiently good to allow pack animals to reach the MILL road crossing, which starts from that point.
    (c) Make the crossing of the ANCRE good for field artillery at Q.36.c.1.3. and Q.36.c.1.7.
    (d) Improve one of the crossings in sub para (a) above, so as to take pack animals.

6. O.C. 19th Welsh Regt. (Pioneers) will place 1 company at disposal of O.C. 123 Field Coy R.E. to assist him in carrying out the work detailed in para 5 (a), (b) and (c). When no longer required by O.C. 123 Field Coy R.E., it will be available for the work detailed in para 8 (a).

7. 151 Field Coy R.E. will
    (a) Make the crossing of the ANCRE good for 60 pdrs at W.11.d.2.6.
    (b) Make the crossing of the ANCRE good for Infantry in single file at W.17.d.1.7.
    (c) Make the crossing of the ANCRE good for Infantry in file and if possible, for Field Artillery at W.28.b.8.5. but work in sub para (a) takes precedence over this.

8. 19th Welsh Regt. will repair the following roads so as to take horse transport, and subsequently, if their condition permits, motor lorries. One company will be employed on each.

   (a) AUTHUILLE – THIEPVAL.
   (b) AVELUY (W.11.d.7.7.) through W.18.a and b – OVILLERS – X.8.b.6.7. – X.9.c.8.9. also from X.8.b.6.7. to R.33.d.8.3.
   (c) ALBERT – BAPAUME road from X.13.d.0.0. north eastwards.

9. The MILL ROAD crossing of the ANCRE (Q.24.a.4.2.) will be made good for field guns by 17th Division and also the road from there to THIEPVAL.

10. The ANCRE crossings detailed in paras 5 and 7 replace those given in 38th Division Order No. 213 para Vll.

Field Coys and Pioneers to acknowledge.

W. Dickinson

Lieut, R.E.
for Lieut. Col. R.E.
C.R.E., 38th (Welsh) Division.

Issued 8.55 p.m.

Copy No. 1. O.C. 123 Field Coy R.E.
"   "   2. O.C. 124 Field Coy R.E.
"   "   3. O.C. 151 Field Coy R.E.
"   "   4. O.C. 19th Welsh Regt.(Pioneers)

For information.

Copy No. 5. 38th Division G.S.
"   "   6. 38th Division A. & Q.
"   "   7. 113 Infantry Brigade.
"   "   8. 114 Infantry Brigade.
"   "   9. 115 Infantry Brigade.
"   "   10. Chief Engineer, Vth Corps.
"   "   11. C.R.E., 17th Division.
"   "   12. C.R.E., 18th Division.
"   "   13. C.R.A., 38th Division.
"   "   14. A.D.M.S., 38th Division.
"   "   15. O.C. 38th M.G.Corps.
"   "   16. War Diary.
"   "   17. File. (C.R.E's copy.)
"   "   18. File.
"   "   19. File.
"   "   20. File.

War Diary

SECRET.   Copy No. 14

38th Division, Royal Engineers.

OPERATION ORDER NO. 68.

Ref. Maps :-   30th August 1918.
Sheets 57.c. & 57.d.
1/40,000.

1. 123rd Field Coy. R.E. will move tomorrow to the neighbourhood of LONGUEVAL, transport to X.10, and take over from O.C. 19th Welsh Regt. (Pioneers) work on the LONGUEVAL - GINCHY - LES BOEUFS Road forward of S.17.b.3.3.

2. O.C. 124th Field Coy. R.E. will take on maintenance of LONGUEVAL - CONTALMAISON Road West of S.17.b.3.3. to meet D.G.T's labour which is working Eastward along the same road from LA BOISELLE. He will also make good the approach road into the Stone Dump in S.14.a.. He will also take charge of the German R.E.Dump at S.14.b.3.8. and issue stores as required.

3. O.C. 151st Field Coy. R.E. will tonight take over from O.C. 123rd Field Coy. R.E. work on the crossing over the River ANCRE at AUTHUILLE and continue this in addition to the work on which he is at present employed at BROOKERS PASS Crossing. (W.11.c. and d.)

4. O.C. 19th Welsh Regt. (Pioneers) will work with two Coys. on the LONGUEVAL - FLERS Road, making it fit for horse transport, and with one Coy. on the BAZENTIN-le-PETIT - MARTINPUICH Road from S.14.b.0.7. to M.32.c.2.8. making it fit for horse transport.

5. All the above work will be carried out under the orders of the C.R.E. 38th Division who will receive instructions from the Chief Engineer Vth Corps as regards work West of LONGUEVAL.

6. When the enemy retires further East the two Coys. of the Pioneers detailed for work on the LONGUEVAL - FLERS Road will probably be required to work in advance of the 123rd Field Coy. R.E., being replaced on the LONGUEVAL - FLERS Road by the Coy. detailed for the BAZENTIN-le-PETIT - MARTINPUICH Road.

7. The Field Coys. working forward (that is from tomorrow 123rd and 124th Field Coys.) will reconnoitre for water

supplies, R.E. Dumps and any other technical matters of interest, reporting useful particulars promptly to C.R.E.

8.   Field Coys. R.E. and Pioneers to acknowledge.

Copy No. 1. O.C. 123rd Field Coy. R.E.
" " 2. O.C. 124th Field Coy. R.E.
" " 3. O.C. 151st Field Coy. R.E.
" " 4. O.C. 19th Welsh Regt. (Pioneers)

For information :-

" " 5. 38th Division "G"
" " 6. 38th Division "A" & "Q"
" " 7. Chief Engineer Vth Corps.
" " 8. 113th Infantry Brigade.
" " 9. 114th Infantry Brigade.
" " 10. 115th Infantry Brigade.
" " 11. C.R.A., 38th Division.
" " 12. 38th Div. Train.
" " 13 A.D.M.S.
" " 14. War Diary.
" " 15. File.

J.E. Kelsall.

Time issued 7.0 p.m.

Lieut. Col. R.E.
C.R.E., 38th Division.

Copy.

Notes on C.R.E., 38th Division Op. Order No.67
dated 23/8/1918.

    Para.5. (a) Q.29.b.8.0. owing to the great difficulty experienced in getting stores forward, the above Bridge was the only one completed in first 24 hours. Bridge takes Infantry in single file. Constructed on cork floats and duckboard connecting bays.
Approx. time starting 9.30 p.m. 23/8/18
      "   "   completion. 2 a.m. 24/8/18
Work also delayed by Infantry crossing while work was in progress.

        Q.24.c.5.0. This bridge was not constructed.

    (b) This was done by Pioneers

AUTHUILLE   (c) This Bridge was started 7.30 p.m. 24/8/18. Completed
CROSSING.   for Field Guns 5 p.m. 25/8/18.

    (d) Was not done.

BROOKERS
PASS.   (a) 23/8/18. 151st able to work here unobserved
       with two sections of ~~sappers~~ and two Platoons of
Para.7.   19th Welsh. Bridge was across gap by 10 a.m.
       24/8/18 but was immediately seriously damaged by hostile shelling. Bridge was completed for Field Guns by 4 p.m. 24/8/18.
       It was decided subsequently that the margin of strength was not sufficient to risk taking 60 pdrs. over this bridge. One extra baulk (standard Field Coy. trestle equipment) had been put under each wheel track of 15 ft. bays making seven baulks in all it being understood that that was the normal procedure to fit bridges for 60 pdrs. But calculations subsequently made threw doubt on the correctness of this especially as it seemed undesirable to consider the timber up to the original quality.

W.17.d.1.7.   (b) Started 3 p.m. 23/8/18 approx. completed 7 p.m. 23/8/18 for Infantry in single file.

W.28.b.8.5.   (c) Started 3 p.m. 23/8/18 approx. complted 10 p.m. 23/8/18 for Infantry in file.

Para.8.

AUTHUILLE - THIEPVAL Road.
    (a) Work was not commenced on this at once as the Pioneers were needed to help with the crossing leading to it. It was subsequently done.

    (b) Reported open for H.T. 26/8/18 at 3 p.m. approx.

    (c) Reported open to lorries to R.36.b.5.5. 26/8/18. The chief obstacle to traffic was a very large mine crater at X.14.b.0.5. which was wider than the road. A temporary way round one side was open for horse traffic by the afternoon of 25th the Corps undertaking the construction of a permanent diversion. The crater was well sited, the road at the point selected running along the face of a slope with a trench running up to the road on the higher side. The temporary way round

P.T.O.

was made on the downhill side of the road by levelling down the crater lip, laying timber crossways with more chalk on top. The whole ground was chalk which facilitated matters. The permanent diversion undertaken by the Corps was on the uphill side of the road.

SECRET   Copy No. 5

38th Division Royal Engineers

OPERATION ORDER NO 66.

Ref. Map :-
Sheet 57.d. 1/40,000.   15th August 1918.

In conjunction with 38th Division Order No. 201.

INFORMATION.

1.   The enemy are reported to have withdrawn to the general line
BUCQUOY - PUISIEUX - R.2.
     It is possible that the enemy may withdraw Eastwards from South
of the River ANCRE also.
     The Division on our left have reached the line - Q.6.central.
Q.12.a.central, and are pushing forward patrols tonight to the spur
in R.2.and towards the general line BATTERY VALLEY - THIEPVAL.
A patrol of that Division crossed the R.ANCRE at Q.24.a.7.3.
unopposed and is being followed by a Battalion whose objective
is R.26.central.
     The enemy still hold a position round ALBERT Cathedral; the
Division on our right is operating against them from the South
and have pushed patrols into W.24.

2.   With a view to testing whether the enemy has withdrawn, 113th
Infantry Brigade will send a Company via AUTHUILLE towards R.31.
central and 115th Infantry Brigade a Company via AVELUY towards
Cross Roads X.13.a.05.30.

3.   If those Companies meet no opposition -

   (a)   The 114th Infantry Brigade will then advance via
   AUTUILLE and AVELUY towards the general line LA - BOISSELLE
   - OVILLERS - LA - BOISSELLE - THIEPVAL, and will make good
   the same. Bde. H.Q. will be at the old Battalion Headquarters
   Q.28.a.9.5.

   (b)   The 115th Infantry Brigade will take over the whole present
   Divisional front and will have the 2nd Battalion 318 American
   Infantry Regiment attached to it in accordance with Warning
   Order GSS 5/109/A.

   (c)   The 113th Infantry Brigade will concentrate in the BROWN
   LINE ready to leap-frog through 114th Brigade to a general
   line - The cutting in X.17.a. - WINDMILL POZIERES and Ridge
   in R.28. West of COURCELETTE.

   A tracing over the 1/20,000 map is attached (Not to Administrative
   Units) shewing in red the tactical points which must be occupied
   by the 114th Infantry Brigade and in blue the points to be occupied
   by 113th Infantry Brigade.

   (d)   The Divisional Artillery (less the present advanced sections)
   will move into position in the PIONEER ROAD - MARTINSART - MESNIL
   VALLEY, 121st Brigade R.F.A. South of MARTINSART 122nd Brigade
   R.F.A.   North of MARTINSART; D.A.C. to HARPONVILLE.
   4 Sections 60 - Prs. and 4 Sections 6" Hows. will also move into
   position in the MARTINSART - MESNIL VALLEY.

4. The following troops will be under the orders of 114th Infantry
Brigade :-
           "D" Coy. 38th Battalion M.G.C. (Major Adamson)

          3 Sections 178th Tunnelling Coy. R.E. (to search for mines etc.)
          E. Squadron 5th Cyclist Regt. (Major Finlay)
          One Field Coy. R.E.

The 114th Brigade will NOT wait for those troops to report before moving. These troops will come under the orders of 113th Brigade when that Brigade passes through 114th Brigade.

5.   The C.R.E., on it being ascertained that 114th Infantry Brigade has crossed the R.ANCRE, will immediately repair the crossings of the R.ANCRE at AVELUY and AUTHUILLE by 2 Coys. R.E. and the 19th Welsh Regt. (Glamorgan Pioneers).

6.   Dumps of ammunition supplies and water will be formed in the MARTINSART VALLEY W.3. W.9.

7.   <u>FIELD COMPANY R.E. INSTRUCTIONS.</u> in the event of para.3. sub. para (a) coming into operation :-

<u>123rd Field Coy. R.E.</u> will repair Bridge and Approach at AUTHUILLE Q.35.d.99.70.
    O.C. 123rd Field Coy. R.E. will get into touch with O.C. 151st Field Coy. R.E. who has had charge of reconnaissance of ANCRE BRIDGES, and will be able to supply information.

<u>151st Field Coy. R.E.</u> will repair Bridge and Approach at AVELUY W.17.b.20.85

<u>19th Welsh Regt. (Pioneers)</u> will repair :-

    (i)   Main BOUZINCOURT - AVELUY Road as far as HAMEL - AVELUY Road. Road to be prepared for rough traffic only in the first instance and then improved afterwards.

    (ii)   MARTINSART - PIONEER Road as far as HAMEL - AVELUY Road

    (iii)   MESNIL - AUTHUILLE Road as far as HAMEL - AVELUY Road.

    (iv)   19th Welsh Welsh Pioneers will assist Field Coys. in making good approaches to bridges if required by R.E. Officers on site.

<u>124th Field Coy. R.E.</u> will get into touch with G.O.C. 114th Infantry Brigade and come under his orders in the event of para.3 sub para. (a) coming into operation, afterwards coming under the orders of G.O.C. 113th Infantry Brigade as in para.4.

    All pontoon equipment and teams to be placed at the disposal of O.C. 151st Field Coy. R.E. for bridging at AVELUY CAUSEWAY.

    O.C. 151st Field Coy. R.E. will arrange time and rendezvous for Pontoon wagons direct with the other Field Coy. Commanders

8.   These orders will be acted upon on the code word "AUCTION" being received from this office.

9.   Divisional Headquarters will not move.

Field Coys. R.E. and Pioneers to acknowledge.

```
Copy No.  1.  O.C. 123rd Field Coy. R.E.
 "   "    2.  O.C. 124th Field Coy. R.E.
 "   "    3.  O.C. 124th Field Coy. R.E.
 "   "    4.  O.C. 19th Welsh Regt. (Pioneers)

          For information :-

 "   "    5.  38th Division "G"
 "   "    6.  38th Division "Q"
 "   "    7.  113th Infantry Brigade.
 "   "    8.  114th Infantry Brigade.
 "   "    9.  115th Infantry Brigade.
 "   "   10.  38th Division R.A.
 "   "   11.  C.E. Vth Corps.
```

J Wood

Time of issue 5 a.m.

Major R.E.
A/C.R.E., 38th Division.

G.S.O. 1	
G.S.O. 2	
G.S.O. 3	
G.S.O. 4	

S E C R E T.

O.C. 124 Field Coy R.E.
38th Divn. G.S. (For information).

      124 Field Coy R.E., less 2 Sections, will accompany 113 Infantry Brigade on Special Operations today, 22nd August, 1918.

      The Company, less 2 Sections, will be at 113 Infantry Brigade Headquarters, V.4.central at 7.0 a.m., under the Command of Major C.H.BRAZEL, R.E., M.C.

      Iron rations to be carried.

      124 Field Coy R.E. to acknowledge.

                         Lieut, R.E.
                       for Lieut. Col. R.E.
22/8/1918.   C.R.E., 38th Division.

Time issued 12.15 a.m.

SECRET.   Copy No. 5

38th Division Royal Engineers

C.R.E's Operation Order No. 67.

23rd August, 1918.

1. The 38th Division together with other troops on both flanks will attack the enemy positions east of the River ANCRE on the night 23/24th August, 1918.
Further particulars and the orders in paras 4 - 10, were communicated verbally to officers Commanding 123 and 151 Field Coys R.E. and O.C. 19th Welsh Regt. (Pioneers) at C.R.E's Conference today.

2. The duties allotted to Field Companies and Pioneers are as under:-

3. 124 Field Coy R.E. has already been detailed as follows :-

    (a) Company, less 2 sections, placed under orders of G.O.C. 113 Infantry Brigade.

    (b) 1 section under orders of G.O.C. 114 Infantry Brigade.

    (c) 1 section under orders of G.O.C. 115 Infantry Brigade.

4. The remaining 2 Field Coys and Divisional Pioneers will work under the orders of the C.R.E. and carry out the following tasks.

5. 123 Field Coy R.E. will

    (a) make crossings of the ANCRE fit for Infantry in single file at :
    Q.29.b.8.0.
    Q.24.c.5.0.
    It is essential that this work be put in hand immediately it is dark enough and completed as soon as possible.
    (b) Make the road from MESNIL through Q.29.a and b to Q.24.a.1.5. sufficiently good to allow pack animals to reach the MILL road crossing, which starts from that point.
    (c) Make the crossing of the ANCRE good for field artillery at Q.36.c.1.3. and Q.36.c.1.7.
    (d) Improve one of the crossings in sub para (a) above, so as to take pack animals.

6. O.C. 19th Welsh Regt. (Pioneers) will place 1 company at disposal of O.C. 123 Field Coy R.E. to assist him in carrying out the work detailed in para 5 (a), (b) and (c). When no longer required by O.C. 123 Field Coy R.E., it will be available for the work detailed in para 8 (a).

7. 151 Field Coy R.E. will
    (a) Make the crossing of the ANCRE good for 60 pdrs at W.11.d.2.6.
    (b) Make the crossing of the ANCRE good for Infantry in single file at W.17.d.1.7.
    (c) Make the crossing of the ANCRE good for Infantry in file and if possible, for Field Artillery at W.28.b.8.5. but work in sub para (a) takes precedence over this.

8. 19th Welsh Regt. will repair the following roads so as to take horse transport, and subsequently, if their condition permits, motor lorries. One company will be employed on each.

   (a) AUTHUILLE - THIEPVAL.
   (b) AVELUY (W.11.d.7.7.) through W.18.a and b - OVILLERS - X.8.b.6.7. - X.9.c.8.9. *also from X.8.b.6.7 to R.33.d.8.3*
   (c) ALBERT - BAPAUME road from X.13.d.0.0. north eastwards.

9. The MILL ROAD crossing of the ANCRE (Q.24.a.4.2.) will be made good for field guns by 17th Division and also the road from there to THIEPVAL.

10. The ANCRE crossings detailed in paras 5 and 7 replace those given in 38th Division Order No. 213 para VII.

Field Coys and Pioneers to acknowledge.

W. Dickinson
Lieut, R.E.
for Lieut. Col. R.E.
Issued 8.55 p.m.   C.R.E., 38th (Welsh) Division.

```
Copy No. 1. O.C. 123 Field Coy R.E.
  "   "  2. O.C. 124 Field Coy R.E.
  "   "  3. O.C. 151 Field Coy R.E.
  "   "  4. O.C. 19th Welsh Regt.(Pioneers)
```

For information.

```
Copy No. 5. 38th Division G.S.
  "   "  6. 38th Division A. & Q.
  "   "  7. 113 Infantry Brigade.
  "   "  8. 114 Infantry Brigade.
  "   "  9. 115 Infantry Brigade.
  "   " 10. Chief Engineer, Vth Corps.
  "   " 11. C.R.E., 17th Division.
  "   " 12. C.R.E., 18th Division.
  "   " 13. C.R.A., 38th Division.
  "   " 14. A.D.M.S., 38th Division.
  "   " 15. O.C. 38th M.G.Corps.
  "   " 16. War Diary.
  "   " 17. File. (C.R.E's copy.)
  "   " 18. File.
  "   " 19. File.
  "   " 20. File.
```

"A" Form.
MESSAGES AND SIGNALS.

Army Form C. 2121.
(In pads of 100.)

Prefix	Code	m	Words	Charge	This message is on a/c of:	Recd. at ...... m.
Office of Origin and Service Instructions.			Sent At ...... m.		...... Service.	Date ......
			To			From ......
			By		(Signature of "Franking Officer.")	By ......

TO: 38th Division G.S.
    38th Division A & Q.

Sender's Number.	Day of Month.	In reply to Number.	AAA
R.E. 4001 f.	23rd		AAA

No change to my R.E. 4001 e. AAA Bridge
Report by 8.0 p

From C.R.E. 38th Div
Place
Time

The above may be forwarded as now corrected. (Z)

38th Division, G.S.
38th Division, A. & Q.

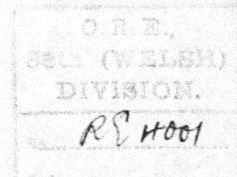

Report on Bridges and River Crossings
over the R. ANCRE up to 2.0 p.m 23/8/18.
****

Serial No.	Nature of Crossing.	Map reference.	Company responsible.	Report as to present state of Bridge and work in hand.
1.	Mill Crossing, HAMEL.	Q.24.a.4.2.	123 Field Coy.	2 Sections are waiting near this spot with material to effect crossings on receipt of orders. Material : Cork floats and pit-props, dumped at the junction of QUAKER ALLEY & metre gauge railway Q.22.a.
2.	Bridge.	Q.29.b.9.1.	123 Field Coy.	Infantry can cross this Bridge with difficulty at present. It will be improved as soon as situation permits.
3.	South CAUSEWAY.	Q.29.d.8.2.	123 Field Coy.	Gap 40 yds wide over main stream. Gap 40 yds wide at Q.30.c.40.15. These gaps will be repaired with Floating Cork Bridges as soon as situation permits.
4.	AUTHUILLE Crossing.	Q.36.c.0.7.	123 Field Coy.	No work has been done on this at present. Material for repairs are dumped in MESNIL pontoons in MARTINSART Wood.
5.	Bridge.	W.11.d.3.6.	151 Field Coy.	Now being repaired.
6.	River Crossing.	W.17.c.8.6.	151 Field Coy.	Tree fitted with wooden hand-rail. Floating bridge 30' long hidden close to this spot. Men are getting ready to have this in position.
7.	River Crossing.	W.17.c.6.0.	151 Field Coy.	Floating bridge is now being put across this point.
8.	Bridge.	W.28.b.8.4.	151 Field Coy.	Reconnaissance now being made of this Bridge.

(No work is possible on Serial Numbers 1 to 4 inc. in day-light.)

                       Dickinson
                             Lieut, R.E.
                      for C.R.E., 38th Division.

23/8/1918.

"A" Form.
MESSAGES AND SIGNALS.

Army Form C. 2121.
(In pads of 100.)

TO	38th Division, G.S.		
	~~38th Division, A. & Q.~~		

Sender's Number.	Day of Month.	In reply to Number.	AAA
R.E. 4001 d	23		

Bridge report to 6.0 p.m AAA Serial No. 5.
AAA 151 Coy report able to work unobserved
AAA Sending 2 sections ~~one~~ sappers and two
Platoons 19th Welsh Pioneers for road clearing
AAA Rest no change AAA

From C.R.E. 38th Divn.

Place

Time

Dickinson Lt. R.E.

"A" Form.
MESSAGES AND SIGNALS.

Army Form C. 2121.
(In pads of 100.)

Prefix......Code......m	Words.	Charge.	This message is on a/c of:	Recd. at......m
Office of Origin and Service Instructions.	Sent At......m		..................Service.	Date............
....	To............			From............
....	By............		(Signature of "Franking Officer.")	By............

TO { ~~125~~
38th Division, G.S.
~~38th Division, A & Q.~~

Sender's Number.	Day of Month.	In reply to Number.	A A A
* R.E. 4001 c.	23		

Bridge report to 5.0 p.m AAA No change AAA

G.S.O. 1
G.S.O. 2
G.S.O. 3
G.S.O. 4

From C.R.E., 38th Divn.
Place
Time

The above may be forwarded as now corrected.   (Z) Dickinson Lt. R.E.
.... Censor.   Signature of Addressor or person authorised to telegraph in his name.

* This line should be erased if not required.

(3198.) Wt. W 12952/M1294. 375,000 Pads. 1/17. H.W.&V., Ld. (E. 818.)

"A" Form.
MESSAGES AND SIGNALS.

Army Form C. 2121.
(In pads of 100.)

| TO | 38th Division, G.S. |

Sender's Number.	Day of Month.	In reply to Number.	AAA
R.E. 4001a	23		

Bridge report to 3.0 p.m AAA No change

3-35/pm

G.S.O. 1
G.S.O. 2
G.S.O. 3
G.S.O. 4

From C.R.E. 38th Divn.
Place
Time

(Z) Dickinson

38th Division, G.S.
38th Division, A. & Q.

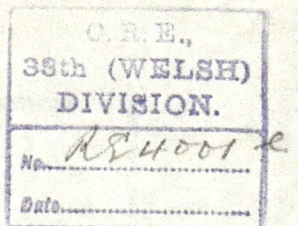

          Bridge report to 7.0 p.m., 23rd instant., together with amendment to Serial list sent under my R.E. 4001 of even date.

Serial No. 1. Work now taken in hand by 17th Division.

Serial No. 2. No change.

Serial No. 3. No work is being done on this Causeway *tonight*

Serial No. 4. No change.

Serial No. 5. No change.

Serial No. 6. No change.

Serial No. 7. No change.

Serial No. 8. Repairs are being taken in hand.

Serial No. 1a. Bridge. Q.24.c.5.0. Coy responsible 123 Field Coy

              Work in hand.— Infantry Bridge is being put

              across here tonight.

                                              Lieut, R.E.
                                    for C.R.E., 38th Division.

23/8/18.

38th Division, G.S.
38th Division, A. & Q.
C.R.A., 38th Division.

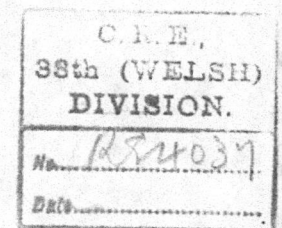

        O.C. 151 Field Coy R.E. reports satisfactory progress on Bridges at BROOKERS PASS, W.11.d.3.6. up to 1.0 a.m.

        River crossings had been finished and defects remedied.

        The enemy retaliation shoots fell on the banks of the river.

        Three bridges well in hand received 4 directs hits.

        Practically all the work done up to 1.0 a.m was thus rendered useless.

        O.C. 151 Field Coy R.E. requires 100 men as extra labour and arrangements have been made with Chief Engineer, Vth Corps to obtain this from 183 Tunnelling Coy R.E.

        O.C. 151 Field Coy R.E. reports work on Artillery Bridge, W.11.d.3.6. should be completed and made passable for Field Guns by 6.0 p.m. this evening.

        Presumably the 3 Bridges reported as having received 4 direct hits are the various gaps in BROOKERS PASS crossing and not the Infantry bridges south of AVELUY.

24/8/18.
                                      Lieut, R.E.
                               for C.R.E., 38th Division.

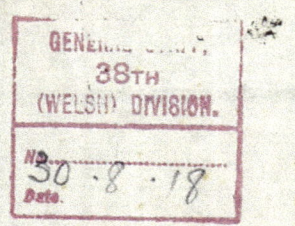
No.
Date 30.8.18

SECRET.   Copy No....... 5

38th Division, Royal Engineers.

OPERATION ORDER NO. 68.

Ref. Maps :-   30th August 1918.
Sheets 57.c. & 57.d.
1/40,000.

1. 123rd Field Coy. R.E. will move tomorrow to the neighbourhood of LONGUEVAL, transport to X.10, and take over from O.C. 19th Welsh Regt. (Pioneers) work on the LONGUEVAL - GINCHY - LES BOEUFS Road forward of S.17.b.3.3.

2. O.C. 124th Field Coy. R.E. will take on maintenance of LONGUEVAL - CONTALMAISON Road West of S.17.b.3.3. to meet D.G.T's labour which is working Eastward along the same road from LA BOISELLE. He will also make good the approach road into the Stone Dump in S.14.a.. He will also take charge of the German R.E.Dump at S.14.b.3.8. and issue stores as required.

3. O.C. 151st Field Coy. R.E. will tonight take over from O.C. 123rd Field Coy. R.E. work on the crossing over the River ANCRE at AUTHUILLE and continue this in addition to the work on which he is at present employed at BROOKERS PASS Crossing. (U.11.c. and d.)

4. O.C. 19th Welsh Regt. (Pioneers) will work with two Coys. on the LONGUEVAL - FLERS Road, making it fit for horse transport, and with one Coy. on the BAZENTIN-le-PETIT - MARTINPUICH Road from S.14.b.0.7. to M.32.c.2.8. making it fit for horse transport.

5. All the above work will be carried out under the orders of the C.R.E. 38th Division who will receive instructions from the Chief Engineer Vth Corps as regards work West of LONGUEVAL.

6. When the enemy retires further East the two Coys. of the Pioneers detailed for work on the LONGUEVAL - FLERS Road will probably be required to work in advance of the 123rd Field Coy. R.E., being replaced on the LONGUEVAL - FLERS Road by the Coy. detailed for the BAZENTIN-le-PETIT - MARTINPUICH Road.

7. The Field Coys. working forward (that is from tomorrow 123rd and 124th Field Coys.) will reconnoitre for water

supplies, R.E. Dumps and any other technical matters of interest, reporting useful particulars promptly to C.R.E.

8.   Field Coys. R.E. and Pioneers to acknowledge.

```
Copy No.  1.  O.C. 123rd Field Coy. R.E.
 "    "   2.  O.C. 124th Field Coy. R.E.
 "    "   3.  O.C. 151st Field Coy. R.E.
 "    "   4.  O.C. 19th Welsh Regt. (Pioneers)

             For information :-

 "    "   5.  38th Division "G"
 "    "   6.  38th Division "A" & "Q"
 "    "   7.  Chief Engineer Vth Corps.
 "    "   8.  113th Infantry Brigade.
 "    "   9.  114th Infantry Brigade.
 "    "  10.  115th Infantry Brigade.
 "    "  11.  C.R.A., 38th Division.
 "    "  12.  38th Div. Train.
 "    "  13.  A.D.M.S.
 "    "  14.  War Diary.
 "    "  15.  File.
```

J.E. Kelsall.
Lieut. Col. R.E.
C.R.E., 38th Division.

Time issued 7.0 p.m.

G.S.O. 1	
G.S.O. 2	
G.S.O. 3	
G.S.O. 4	

171. Wt.W.202/W.P.2212. 300,000(2). 4/20. S.O.,F.Rd.

COVER

FOR

BRANCH MEMORANDA.

Unregistered.

Referred to	Date	Referred to	Date

Instructions regarding War Diaries and Intelligence Summaries are contained in F.S. Regs., Part II. and the Staff Manual respectively. Title Pages will be prepared in manuscript.

Army Form C. 2118

WAR DIARY
or
INTELLIGENCE SUMMARY
(Erase heading not required.)

Headquarters,
38th Division, Royal Engineers.
September 1918 (4 Sheets. Sheet 1.)

Place	Date	Hour	Summary of Events and Information	Remarks and references to Appendices
USNA REDOUBT (W.24.b. 3.7.Sheet 57.D.)	1st.		R.E. Headquarters moved from USNA REDOUBT to CONTALMAISON (Tents and bivouacs).	
CONTALMAISON. (X.16.a.9.9. Sheet 57.D.)	1st-3rd.		Work was continued on roads and bridges over R.ANCRE by the three Field Coys. and Pioneers, as follows:- 123rd Field Coy. R.E. on AUTHUILLE CROSSING, 151st Field Coy. R.E. on BROOKER PASS (AVELUY) CROSSING, 124th Field Coy. R.E. and Pioneers on roads. On 3rd inst. 151st Field Coy. R.E. took over work on AUTHUILLE CROSSING from 123rd Field Coy. R.E. the latter being placed under the orders of 114th Infantry Brigade as part of the advanced guard and moving forward accordingly.	C.R.E.,Op. Order No. 69 d/2/9/18 attached.
LESBOEUFS (T.4.c.0.4. Sheet 57.C)	3rd-11th.		R.E., Headquarters moved from CONTALMAISON to LES BOEUFS (tents.)	
	4th.		The advanced guard crossed the CANAL DU NORD near MANANCOURT. During the night 4th/5th 123rd Field Coy. R.E. constructed a light pontoon bridge part way across at V.8.c.7.3. Sheet 57.C.but as 7 half pontoons were required, the Company equipment was not sufficient. Various reports on crossings were received from O.C. 123rd Field Coy. R.E.	
	5th		At 7.30 a.m. C.R.E. received telephone report from O.C. 123rd Field Coy. R.E. that he needed more pontoons to complete light bridge at V.8.c.7.3. and also further pontoons for a medium bridge ordered by G.S.O.1 near same place, also that his Officers and men were done up, there having been a lot of gas in the valley during the night. Orders were at once issued for 151st Field Coy. R.E. with its personnel to place itself at disposal of O.C. 123rd Field Coy. R.E. The Pontoons of 124th Field Coy. R.E. were ordered up and Chief Engineer, Vth Corps was asked to send up 6 pontoons from the No.3.Pontoon Park. During the afternoon C.R.E. personally reconnoitred the crossings of CANAL DU NORD with following results :- (1) MANANCOURT BRIDGE. V.13.d.5.2., broken, but as the canal was not dug to full dimensions there, was resting on the ground, and with a little work on approaches and roadway would take probably any traffic. Alongside it on the S.E. sidewas a timber cribwork	

WAR DIARY
or
INTELLIGENCE SUMMARY

Headquarters,
38th Division, Royal Engineers.

Sheet 2/4

Army Form C. 2118

(Erase heading not required.)

Instructions regarding War Diaries and Intelligence Summaries are contained in F.S. Regs., Part II. and the Staff Manual respectively. Title Pages will be prepared in manuscript.

Place	Date	Hour	Summary of Events and Information	Remarks and references to Appendices
			causeway fit for at least field guns. Work had been recently done on this (said to be by 12th Division on right of 38th Division). N.E. of this canal was full of water about 120 feet wide.	
			(2) German footbridge for Infantry in single file intact at V.14.a.3.7.	
			(3) Girder bridge at V.13.a.5.9. demolished (apparently Not recently) A timber bridge built up on top of the fallen girders had been destroyed. Could be easily rebuilt for Field Guns.	
			(4) At V.8.c.7.3. the partly built light pontoon bridge built the night before by 123rd Field Coy.	
			(5) The road bridge at V.8.b.4.5. was demolished, but 77th Field Coy. R.E. (17th Division - on left of 38th Division) was rebuilding with timber lattice girders.	
			Owing to enemy observation pontoons could not be taken to Canal Bank till dusk. On night 5th/6th the light pontoon bridge at V.8.c.7.3. was completed and a medium pontoon bridge constructed about 50 yards further N.E. The approaches did not permit of this being used by wheeled traffic. (Note: the bridge referred to at (3) above was not rebuilt, as G.S.O.1 had ordered the medium pontoon bridge instead) On 5th and night 5th/6th the 38th Division was relieved by 21st Division, R.E. Headquarters remaining at LESBOEUFS. While out of the line two Field Company sections were organised for forward water work, when the Division next went forward, to work directly under C.R.E. reconnoitring for water supplies and putting them in order. The three Field Coys. moved to BEAULENCOURT to work on the Divisional Reception Camp there.	
ETRICOURT	11th – 21st.		Division and R.E. Headquarters moved from LESBOEUFS to huts at ETRICOURT. 124th and 151st Field Coys. moved forward same day and worked on huts for Brigades and Divisional Headquarters respectively.	
	12th		123rd Field Coy. moved forward. Except for some parties repairing huts, all three Field Coys. and Pioneers were employed on road repair and maintenance.	

Army Form C. 2118

WAR DIARY
or
INTELLIGENCE SUMMARY

(Erase heading not required.)

Headquarters,
38th Division, Royal Engineers.
Sheet 3/4

Instructions regarding War Diaries and Intelligence Summaries are contained in F.S. Regs., Part II. and the Staff Manual respectively. Title Pages will be prepared in manuscript.

Place	Date	Hour	Summary of Events and Information	Remarks and references to Appendices
ETRICOURT	(Contd.) 15th.		Two Sections of 175 Tunnelling Coy. R.E. which had been employed under Brigades examining dug-outs etc., came under orders of C.R.E., for work on dugouts in W.3.a. sheet 57.C. which were required for Battle Headquarters for 113th and 114th Infantry Brigades and C.R.A. C.R.E. arranged for 124th Field Coy. to construct splinter proof details on spot and also arranged for 124th Field Coy. for use as shelters at same place and to repair and improve existing dugouts in forward area for use as Battalion Headquarters etc. also for 151st Field Coy. to repair a light railway in W.2.3 and 4 Sheet 57.C. From 16/9/18 inclusive the Divisional Pioneers were placed at disposal of these Coys., two Coys. Pioneers with 124th Field Coy., 1 Coy. Pioneers with 151st Field Coy. Two Sections of 123rd Field Coy. R.E. were also placed at disposal of 124th Field Coy. R.E. from 16/9/18 inclusive. The above work was finished on the evening of 17th in readiness for an attack to be made next morning.	Copy of C. R.E.38th Div No.R.E.793 d/10/9/18 (orders for Field Coys & Pioneers) attached.
	18th		Attack by 38th Division (113th and 114th Infantry Brigades) in conjunction with Divisions on both flanks. One Coy. of 19th Welsh Regt. (Pioneers) was placed at disposal of each Brigade for consolidation. The Chief obstacles on the FINS - GOUZEAUCOURT road were three craters which the enemy had blown at W.2.c.6.2., W.4.b.2.7. and W.5.a.1.9. These all completely blocked the road. The first had had roadways made good on both sides prior to 38th Division taking over. These were improved before 18th and the crater was completely filled in by evening of 18th. The other two had roadways made round them before 18th and were improved subsequently. That at W.5.a.1.9. being in what was (up to 18th) our front line, not much work could be done, before 18th. It is considered that the quickest way of getting a road open for traffic where a crater has been blown, would sometimes be by bridging, the crater being subsequently filled in round the bridge supports.	C.R.E.,38th Div. Op.Or. No.71.d/16 /9/18 attd.
	19th		From the night 14th/15th onwards there was a good deal of shelling near Divisional Headquarters by H.V.Guns and in consequence Div. H.Q. except "G" and R.E. moved back on 17th to 0.36.c. Sheet 57.C. A certain number of R.E. were employed putting huts there into repair. (R.E. H.Q. Staff slept in existing dugouts adjoining their huts at ETRICOURT). Field Coys. were employed chiefly on road work and repairs to rear Divisional Headquarters at 0.36.c. In the afternoon the Divisional Commander ordered a Field Coy. to be employed that night digging strong points etc. in our front line North of the FINS - GOUZEAUCOURT road, as required by the Battalion Commander. The only Coy. that could be got there in time was 151st	

Headquarters,
38th Division, Royal Engineers.

WAR DIARY
or
INTELLIGENCE SUMMARY

(Sheet 4/4)

(Erase heading not required.)

Army Form C. 2118

Instructions regarding War Diaries and Intelligence Summaries are contained in F.S. Regs., Part II. and the Staff Manual respectively. Title Pages will be prepared in manuscript.

Place	Date	Hour	Summary of Events and Information	Remarks and references to Appendices
Near BUS.	20th–28th.		which was working on the FINS- GOUZEAUCOURT road. On night 19th/20th the 17th Division took over from the Right Brigade of 38th Division and on night 20th/21st took over the remainder of the Division front. On 21st the Division H.Q. moved to huts at 0.36.c.1.8.Sheet 57.C. and R.E.H.Q. to a quarry about 700 yards North at 0.30.c.15.15. (hut and dugouts) Field Coys. were in part employed on miscellaneous jobs, making Divisional H.Qrs. and Brigades more comfortable.	
Near FINS.	28th–30th		Division and R.E., H.Q. moved on 28th to huts at V.18.c.1.9. Sheet 57.c. near (FINS)in readiness to go forward in connection with operations. Major Brazel R.E.,O.C. 124th Field Coy. R.E. went to H.Q., C.R.E. 18th Division at LIERMONT on 28th as R.E. Liaison officer. Field Coys. and Pioneers moved on 28th to near HEUDECOURT. Pioneers employed from 28th inclusive on making good tracks East and North East of HEUDECOURT.	Copy of C.R.E. Op. Order No.72 d/18/9/18 attached

1st October 1918.

T.S. Evean.

Lieut. Col. R.E.
C.R.E., 38th Division.

Instructions regarding War Diaries and Intelligence
Summaries are contained in F. S. Regs., Part II.
and the Staff Manual respectively. Title pages
will be prepared in manuscript.

WAR DIARY
or
INTELLIGENCE SUMMARY

Headquarters,
38th Division, Royal Engineers,
October, 1918. (5 Sheets. Sheet. 1.)

(Erase heading not required.)

Army Form C. 2118.

Vol. 34.

Place	Date	Hour	Summary of Events and Information	Remarks and references to Appendices
Near FINS.	1st to 4th		Division and R.E., H.Q. in field at V.18.c.1.9. Sheet 57.c. Field Companies and Pioneers employed on various jobs, improving huts, hutting etc. When 50th Division relieved 18th Division on right of 38th Division (end of September or early in October) Major Brazel, R.E. remained at LIERMONT with C.R.E., 50th Division as R.E. Liaison Officer.	
EPEHY.	4th to 7th.		Division and R.E., H.Q. moved on 4th from near FINS to dugouts in railway embankment at F.1.d.8.8. Sheet 62.c., improvements being effected to the accommodation there during the morning by 124th Field Coy. R.E.	
	5.		Major Brazel R.E. rejoined his Company (124th Field Coy. R.E.) from acting as R.E. Liaison Officer with C.R.E., 50th Division. Site near OSSUS was chosen for trestle bridges to be erected over CANAL D'ESCAUT and adjoining stream, by 124th Field Coy. R.E. A good deal of excavation through the banks was necessary for the approaches and this work was done by the Pioneers. Eventually two bridges were constructed side by side over the canal at S.25.b.5.7. Sheet 57.b., both being for Infantry in fours and Field Artillery. One was for East bound traffic the other for West bound. Each was a five bay Weldon Trestle Bridge, mud sills being secured to the trestle legs just above the foot plates. The bridges over the stream on East side were about 16 feet span supported at the centre on 6" round piles. The approaches to the bridges were cross country tracks only, which were marked out with pickets by the Pioneers. The track on the Eastern bank joined the road at S.20.b.0.8. Where the approaches to the bridge were cut through the banks, the ground was very soft and slabbing had to be laid. This was done by the Pioneers. The first bridge was open for traffic at 15.00 hours. The second bridge was never opened for traffic owing to delay in supply of slabs for the approaches; the work was otherwise complete. Meantime 123rd and 151st Field Coys. were placed under orders of Infantry Brigades by Divisional orders and went forward with the Brigades. On 7th the Division ordered two Sections of 124th Field Company to be placed under orders of 114th Infantry Brigade for a special consolidation job next day. On completion they again came under C.R.E's orders. Watering points for horses being required at Canal D'Escaut, two sections were withdrawn from Field Companies with Brigades, by Divisional orders, to be under C.R.E's orders for this and similar work in future (One Section from 123rd Field Coy. - One Section from 151st Field Coy)	

Headquarters,
38th Division Royal Engineers. Army Form C. 2118.

WAR DIARY

INTELLIGENCE SUMMARY.   October 1918 (5 Sheets. Sheet 2.)

(Erase heading not required.)

Place	Date	Hour	Summary of Events and Information	Remarks and references to Appendices
	6th		C.R.E. and Camp Commandant, Divisional H.Qrs., reconnoitred for new Divisional and R.E.,H.Q. and selected site in HINDENBURG line in S.21.d. Sheet 57.b. where there were dugouts.	
	7th.		The two water sections were employed improving new Divisional and R.E.,H.Qrs.	
HINDENBURG LINE near VENDHUILLE	7th to 10th.		Divisional and R.E.,Hqrs. moved on 7th from EPEHY to dugouts in S.21.d. sheet 57.b. The R.E.,H.Q. being very cramped R.E.,H.Q. moved on 8th to better dugouts about 500 yards further South, which had been vacated by other troops the evening before.	
	9th.		123rd and 151st Field Coys. came under orders of C.R.E. again and all Field Coys. and Pioneers were employed on road repairs. Large road craters were dealt with at T.10.c.8.8, T.5.c.2.4. 0.23.c.8.2. and 0.28.b.7.2. (all sheet 57.b.)	
VILLERS OUTREAUX.	10th to 11th		On 10th Division and R.E.,H.Qrs. moved from HINDENBURG LINE to VILLERS OUTREAUX (occupying houses) 123rd Field Coy. R.E. was placed under orders of C.E.,Vth Corps to prepare new Corps H.Qrs. at SALVIGNY, coming again under C.R.E's orders on 13th.	
CLARY.	11th to 12th		On 11th, Division and R.E.,H.Q. moved from VILLERS OUTREAUX to CLARY (occupying houses)	
BERTRY	12th to 24th		On 12th, Division and R.E.,H.Q. moved from CLARY to BERTRY. By 13th all three Field Coys. and Pioneers were concentrated in BERTRY and TROISVILLES and parties were employed clearing mud off roads and improving them	
	12th		38th Division relieved 33rd Division and C.R.E. took over maintenance of footbridges over River SELLE, within Divisional boundaries. Twelve light pontoon bridges had been built by C.R.E. 33rd Division. Two of these were unserviceable and the remaining ten are numbered 14 - 22 and 22.a. on the attached tracing. Copy attached of C.R.E.,38th Division R.E.5597 "Report on bridges over River SELLE on 20/10/18 (1 memo. and 1 tracing) 151st Field Coy. R.E. was placed under the orders of G.O.C. 115th Infantry Brigade, in line.	

WAR DIARY

Headquarters,
38th Division, Royal Engineers.

INTELLIGENCE SUMMARY. October 1918. (5 Sheets. Sheet 3).

Instructions regarding War Diaries and Intelligence Summaries are contained in F.S. Regs. Part II. and the Staff Manual respectively. Title pages will be prepared in manuscript.

Army Form C. 2118.

Place	Date	Hour	Summary of Events and Information	Remarks and references to Appendices
	14th to 22nd		An attack by 38th Division and by 17th Division on its left having been fixed for 20th (zero 02.00 hours) the following are the particulars of R.E. work, as finally settled after various changes :- (1) 24 footbridges (including those existing) were required to be in position in time to allow the attacking troops to form up on the East side of the river prior to zero. Any additional footbridges possible to be made. This work was allotted to 123rd Field Coy. R.E. and on night 18/19th part was transferred to 151st Field Coy. R.E., who had meantime been withdrawn from 115th Infantry Brigade and placed under orders of C.R.E. The right Divisional boundary was shifted Southwards prior to the attack, ground being taken over from 66th Division. The 24 bridges were completed by night 18/19th and are numbered 1 - 24 on attached tracing.* There were in addition 4 other footbridges numbered O.O.a., and 22.a. After dusk on 19th, 24 of the footbridges had tapes laid back from them to the road which runs parallel to the river through K.15.c and d., K.21.b., and K.22.a. and c. Where these tapes met the road, boards were erected with numbers painted in luminous paint corresponding to the numbers of the bridges. (2) The possibility of making a crossing for tanks to use during the attack was raised on 14th instant by "G" of 38th Division. Timber crib work was suggested by the Tank Officer and he came to see C.R.E. that afternoon to discuss the question. O.C. 123rd Field Coy. R.E. and a Tank Officer reconnoitred the site after dark on 15th. The work was decided on and was entrusted to 123rd Field Coy. R.E. The attached sketch shews what was done. Lieut. Doyle was in charge of the job and the job was completed by night 18/19th. The position of the crossing was indicated by a board on each flank on both sides of the river, the Western faces of the boards being painted white, the boards themselves being screened from the enemy. Tanks crossed successfully. A returning tank had some difficulty in getting up the Western bank of the river (which was higher than the Eastern at this crossing) but a sleeper placed across under the tracks enabled them to get the necessary grip. The crossing is marked on attached footbridges and tank crossing tracing. The work on the bridges and tank crossing was carried out under very difficult and dangerous conditions. All stores had to be transported down forward slopes, which were shelled and the enemy's posts were in some cases West of the road which runs between the railway and the river, and his sentries were very alert. That the work was so	* Copy attached of C.R.E. 38th Div. R.E. 5597 "Report on Bridges over R. SELLE on 20/10/18" (1 memo & 1 tracing)

WAR DIARY
or
INTELLIGENCE SUMMARY

Headquarters, 38th Division
Royal Engineers,

October 1918. (5 Sheets. Sheet 4.)

Army Form C. 2118.

Place	Date	Hour	Summary of Events and Information	Remarks and references to Appendices
			(3) successfully completed reflects great credit on all concerned. After zero two bridges for field artillery had to be constructed. This work was done by 123rd Field Coy. One was formed by decking the tank crossing: the other was a medium pontoon bridge of two bays. A second medium pontoon bridge was also erected, thus giving three horse transport bridges. All three were close together and the pontoon bridges were marked "H.T." on the attached tracing * 123rd Field Coy. R.E. having suffered considerable casualties when starting these bridges, the work was delayed. O.C. 151st Field Coy. R.E. was therefore ordered at 11.35 hours to place two sections of his Company at the disposal of 123rd Field Coy. R.E. and with their assistance the work was finished same day.	
			(4) A bridge for all arms including tanks had to be erected after zero on 20th over the River SELLE at MONTAY (K.22.d.4.5. Sheet 57.b.) where the masonry bridge had been blown. This work was allotted to 124th Field Coy. R.E. Stores for two standard spans (22 ft. girders each span) and sleepers for crib work were delivered some days beforehand at a bridging dump which was formed at J.30.c.2.8. Sheet 57.b. Here they were very carefully sorted out and marked by the Company so that there would be no delay when the time for erecting came. On the morning of the 20th the necessary reconnaissance was made under shell and M.G.fire and by 10.10 hours orders were sent for the Company to proceed to the site from the bridging dump. Work was started preparing site at 13.15 hours. The lower portion of the crib pier for the centre support was put together on shore, floated to position and sunk. The bridge was available for traffic by 16.30 hours 21st. Work was suspended for about 5 hours during night 20/21st. Some further work was done to the approaches on 22nd. C.R.E., Vth Corps put a rectangular Inglis bridge across, alongside the above bridge so as to make a double traffic route.	
			(5) A bridge for all traffic including tanks had to be erected over the River SELLE where a masonry bridge had been blown at K.22.a.8.1. 212th Field Coy. R.E. of 33rd Division was placed under the orders of C.R.E. 38th Division for this work. A 30 ft. span reinforced bridge had been delivered at a bridging dump at P.17.a.9.2. Sheet 57.b. by XIII Corps, in whose area the bridge site was, up to a few days before the attack. This bridge was placed at the disposal of C.R.E., 38th Division for the job. On the morning of 20th the necessary measurements were taken under shell fire and work started at 12.45 hours,	

WAR DIARY

INTELLIGENCE SUMMARY

Headquarters,
38th Division, Royal Engineers. Army Form C. 2118.

October 1918. (5 Sheets. Sheet 5.)

Place	Date	Hour	Summary of Events and Information	Remarks and references to Appendices
			and the bridge was completed at 08.45 hours on 21st. Shelling caused delay. Battle	
	21st and 22nd.		(6) Work was done for a few days prior to the 20th in making Headquarters for two Infantry Brigades in the road bank at J.25.d.6.5. Sheet 57.b. Elephant shelters and mined dugouts etc. were made. This work was done by Pioneers and 124th Field Coy. R.E. Work was done improving the approaches to the horse transport bridges over River SELLE and in making routes from them to the East side of the railway, which being in cuttings and on embankments formed a serious obstacle. Pioneers and 123rd and 151st Field Coys. were employed on this. The debris of the railway bridge at K.22.d.8.8. which had been blown on to the MONTAY - FOREST road, was also cleared as far as time would allow. The above work was urgent, as 33rd Division had to pass through 38th Division on night 22nd/23rd and attack next day, the 38th Division following up. All the bridges constructed by the 38th Division proved entirely satisfactory.	
	23rd		33rd Division attacked and advanced line to near ENGLEFONTAINE. 151st Field Coy. R.E. (less water section) placed under orders of 115th Infantry Brigade.	
MONTAY	24th to 25th.		Division and R.E., H.Q. moved to MONTAY on 24th.	
FOREST	25th to 31st		On 25th R.E., H.Q. moved to FOREST, Division H.Q. moving same day to RICHEMONT (K.5.d. Sheet 57.b) On 26th 38th Division relieved 33rd Division, 115th Infantry Brigade in the line, the 33rd Division having meantime captured ENGLEFONTAINE. 123rd Field Coy. R.E. was placed under orders of G.O.C. 115th Infantry Brigade to assist him in consolidating. He thus had two Field Coys. (each less 1 Section on water supply). Owing to men on leave, casualties and sickness, these Companies were so weak that two sections of 124th Field Coy. R.E. were, on 26th, placed under orders of O.C. 123rd Field Coy. R.E. and O.C. 151st Field Coy. R.E. (one section under each). These sections were withdrawn and rejoined their own Company on 31st/10/18. 123rd Field Coy. R.E. was withdrawn from being under G.O.C. 115th Infantry Brigade on 31/10/18 and came under the orders of C.R.E.	

T. E. Kinsall,
Lieut. Col. R.E.
G.R.E., 38th Division.

2/11/18.

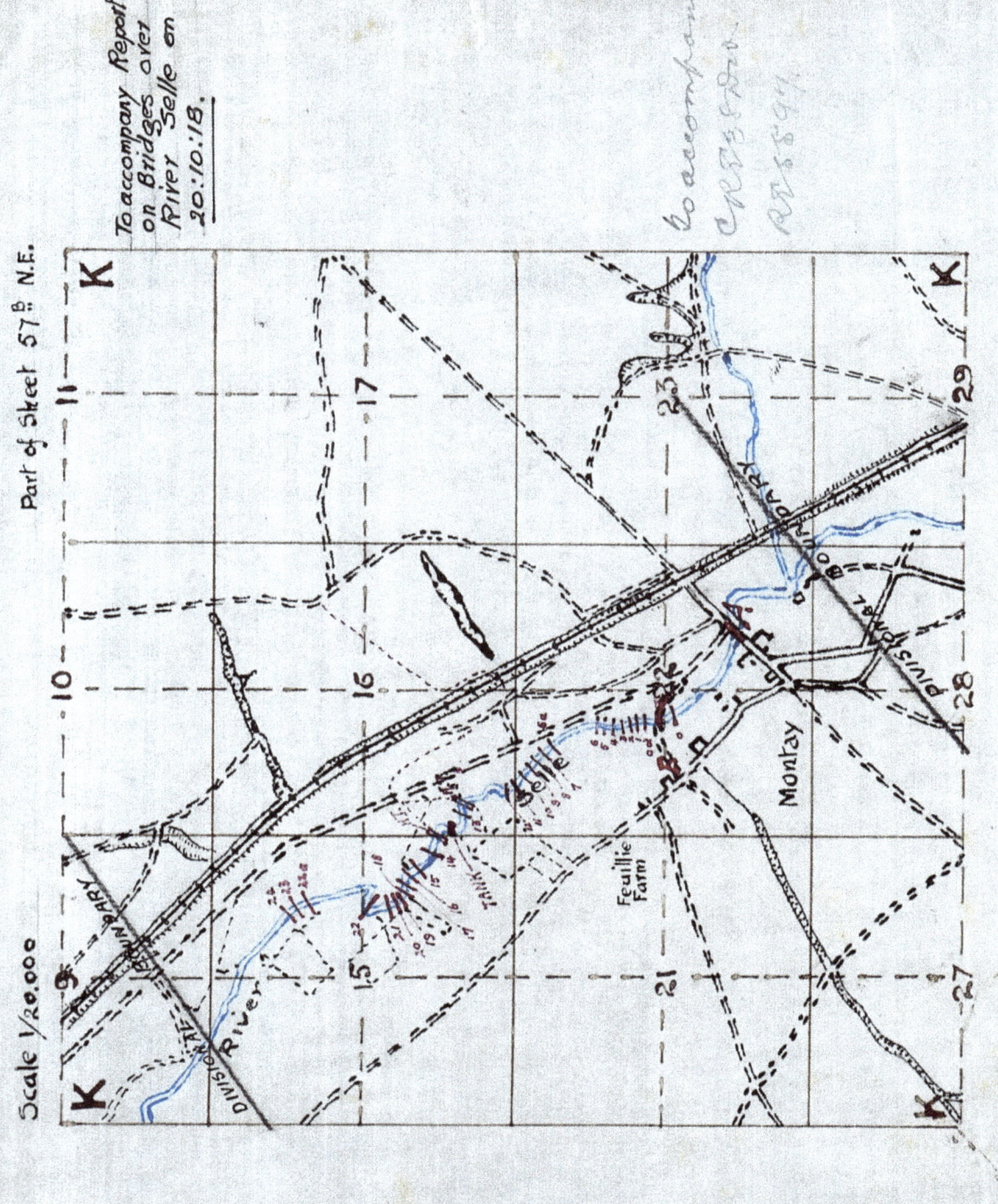

C.R.E., 38th Division R.E.5597

REPORT ON BRIDGES OVER RIVER SELLE ON 20/10/1918.

(See attached tracing)

A. Two heavy bridges side by side under construction. S.E. one for all traffic except tanks. N.W. one for all traffic including tanks.

B. Heavy bridge for all traffic including tanks.

O. Barrel pier footbridge.

O.a. Barrel pier footbridge.

```
*     1.   Cork float footbridge.
*     2    "     "     "
*     3    "     "     "
*     4    "     "     "
*     5    "     "     "
*     6    "     "     "
      6a.  "     "     "
*     7    "     "     "
*     8    "     "     "
*     9    "     "     "
*     10   "     "     "
*     11   "     "     "
*     12   "     "     "
      -    Pontoon bridge for Field Artillery.
*     13   Cork float footbridge.
      -    Tank crossing.
      -    Pontoon bridge for Field Artillery.
ø *   14   Pontoon bridge.
  *   15      "      "     (damaged)
  *   16      "      "     (  "   )
ø *   17      "      "
ø *   18      "      "
ø *   19      "      "
      20      "      "
ø *   21      "      "
ø *   22      "      "
ø *   22a.    "      "
  *   23   Cork footbridge (damaged)
  *   24      "      "    (  "   )
```

* Approach marked by tape.
ø Will take pack animals with care.

Note :- Damaged footbridges are being repaired.

(Sd) ᴛ?ᴋ.

To :- 38th Division "G"
C.R.E., 33rd Division.
C.E., Vth Corps.

Lieut. Col. R.E.
C.R.E., 38th Division.

CRIB TANK CROSSING OVER RIVER SELLE AT K.16.C.05.45. Sheet 57 R

Built of Railway Sleepers

SCALE 4 Feet to an inch

SECTION AA

3'-9" 19'-6" 10'-0" Water level

Bolts

Packing pieces

SECTION BB

Water level 17'-0" 3'-6½" 3'-5"

Packing piece 12 foot Bottom of river is gritty

PLAN

The timbers of the Crib were held in position by 1½" diam. rods which were driven into the bottom of the river. The Crib was built up on the surface of the water, the sleepers being bored and fitted over the rods until the required height was attained, 12 inches being allowed for sinkage under the weight of the Tank. The Crib was then weighted to keep it in position.

a.a.a. blocks between Sleepers

Bolts

17'-0" 10'-0" 9'-6"

1½" rods

Packing piece

22-10-18 C.R.E.

G.O.C.   TAC

Attached arrangements do
not give the dropping
station at Adv. Brigade
H.Q. nor the arrangements
for Tank Wireless.
McClintock is coming to see
me directly and I will
then let Brigades know
both the above.

R.A.F. know the position
of our Adv. Bde. H.Q.
but I am ensuring that
they drop there as well as
at Adv. Div. Report Centre.
(They have been asked to do
this as a general rule.)

17.10.18   J.S.M.

Attached went out to Brigadiers
as well as Signal Sections

Signal Arrangements for 20th

Lines

Two Infantry Divisions laid by Divl. HQ Sigs exist from 115 MG LEFAYT to Battle HQ K25 D.7.4. One of these lines to be diverted to 114 MG LEFAYT on morning 18th by DHQ Sigs.

These lines will be extended to Hill top (corner of fence) about K20.d.2.8 in D5 cable by DHQ Sigs on 18th and extended by the 114 Bde Sigs to Battle HQ. K20.b.2.3 on night 18/19th.

At present these two lines are cut at K25.c.5.9 and one joined to DIV. OBS. at K19.d.4.8 and one to Battery of 115 Bde at J30.a.9.6 but they will be joined through when required (at K25.C.5.9) to K25.d.7.4 by Divl HQ Linesmen.

A Lateral exists between group & 114 and 115 HQ and a direct line from DHQ to each of 113, 114 & 115 present HQ.

RA LINES

On night of 19/20 the R.F.A. Bde Comdrs. of 121 & 122 Bdes will be at K25.d.7.4 with 113 & 114 Bde Battle HQ and each will have a direct line to his own R.F.A. Bde HQ. The CRA at DHQ will also have one line from DHQ to those two

RFA Bde Comdrs. direct from RA.HQ.
Exchange at P4.b.8.8.

From the RA adv Exchge direct lines will go to each RFA Bde te. the HE Infy Bde HQ's in LE FAYT. Laid by DA Sigs.

FLANK DIVS.

A direct line exists from 38 DHQ to each of 17 and 66 DHQ's: one from 38 DHQ to Adv. 66 Div at P4.b.2.0. From this point a line also exists via 38 DA Adv Exch: to 115 HQ.

WIRELESS

Directing Stn at DIV HQ working to Trench Set at BATTLE HQ K25.d.7.4 (to be handed over by 115 Bde to 114). Each of 114 & 113 Bdes will be allotted one pair of loop sets for use as required.

The rear loop set if at the same place as the Trench set must be in the same shelter. W/T/O will arrange.

VISUAL

No details yet arranged and it is doubtful if any visual can be arranged behind Bde HQ's.

MESSAGE ROCKETS

are being issued to 113 & 114 Bdes primarily for use back across the River SELLE. K.20.b.8.3 will probably be a suitable target.

AEROPLANE DROPPING STATION.

will be near 115 HQ LE FAYT (?). will keep a look out and transmit messages to DIV. HQ.

PIGEONS

Loft at ETRICOURT 1½ hrs flight. 12 birds will be available for 20th, and will be allotted – 6 each to 113 & 114 Bdes.

C. J. Aston
Major RE
O/c 38 Div Signal Co.

38th DIVISIONAL SIGNAL COMPANY
No. 7619
Date 17.10.18

38 DIV. COMMUNICATIONS TRUNK LINE DIAGRAM. ON 20:10:18

Add:
G
113 Bde + Sigs:
114 " "
115 " "
~~Lieut Richardson~~
Div Arty.

Addendum to Signal Arrangements for 20 Oct.

1. Dropping Station

An additional dropping station has been arranged at Adv. Bde HQ K.25.d.7.4. Duplicate messages will be dropped there and at the TROISVILLE Station which is at P.4.B.8.6.

2. Wireless.

The Tanks have wireless communication as follows (by C.W.):—

Between O.C. Tanks at Div HQ and a station at K.25.d.7.4*

Also between either of these stations and a Tank used by Div Observers.

Div. Obs. also have a forward loop set communicating to Bde HQ at K.25.d.7.4. If necessary via one of the forward loop sets with Battalions.

3. A telephone line is also laid to the Balloon at BERTRY Stn.

* O/C Tanks is arranging to have his station in the vicinity of Adv. Bde HQ.

WAR DIARY

INTELLIGENCE SUMMARY

Army Form C. 2118.

Headquarters,
38th Division R.E.

Sheets 2
Sheet No. 1.

November/918

Place	Date	Hour	Summary of Events and Information	Remarks and References to Appendices
FOREST.	1st. - 5th.		Divisional Conference on 1st reference attack arranged for 4th. Chief Engineer, Vth Corps held a conference of C.R.E's at OVILLERS on 2nd to arrange engineering questions for the attack. The same afternoon C.R.E., 38th Division held a conference of Field Company Commanders and O.C. Pioneers to settle details. O.C. 151 Field Coy R.E. with one Company Pioneers under his orders was given a roving commission under C.R.E. to reconnoitre and do preliminary clearing of routes, special attention being paid to assisting Cable signal wagon and guns to get forward. One company Pioneers and two sections of Field Coy R.E. were ordered to do such reconnaissance of route "B" as was possible and get to work on it.	Engineer Instructions Appendix 'B' of Vth Corps Operation Order No. 239 att.)
	4th.		Attack by 38th Division in conjunction with Division on both flanks. At noon C.R.E. moved forward to ENGLEFONTAINE, calling en route Pioneers and 123 and 124 Field Coys R.E.(who were S.W. of BOIS DE VENDIGIES), and ordering them to ENGLEFONTAINE. The attack went very well and a blown culvert at A.2.d.2.0. (sheet 57.A.) was repaired before dark by 124 Field Coy R.E. They improved this crossing next day. 123 Field Coy R.E. made a diversion round a Crater at A.10.a.9.0. (sheet 57.A.) and next day made good the road. After dark, a report was received that there was a crater at A.11.a.6.5. (sheet 57.A.) and a party of Pioneers were sent out to deal with it. They found, however, that troops of another Division were working on a diversion. Next day traffic crossed by the Diversion, and 124 Field Coy R.E. made good the road over the crater on 5th and 6th.	
LOCQUIGNOL.	5th. - 7th.		On 5th Division and R.E.H.Qrs moved from FOREST to LOCQUIGNOL. On 5th and 6th all Field Companies and Pioneers were employed on road work. The road from ENGLEFONTAINE via A.9.c. and B.1.b. (sheet 57.A.) to LOCQUIGNOL was only fit for Horse Transport the metalling was badly worn and covered with mud and some shell holes needed repair, so that there was much work to be done. This was rendered more difficult by the endless stream of transport passing along the road. The 5th and 6th being very wet days, added to the difficulties.	
BERLAIMONT.	7th. - 8th.		On 7th Field Coy and Pioneer Commanders met C.R.E. at LOCQUIGNOL to get orders for work. Their Companies being on the move that day, to billets and bivouacs near the River SAMBRE. 123rd Field Coy R.E. was detailed to make good a crater at C.4.d.2.6., 124th Field Coy R.E. to assist 222nd Field Coy R.E. of 33rd Division with an Artillery trestle bridge at C.14.b.3.7., 151st Field Coy R.E. to complete a detour past crater at B.10.b.2.5., and Pioneers to work on roads. Owing to delays due to traffic on the road, all work was not completed. Division H.Qrs moved on 7th to AULNOYE and R.E.H.Qrs to BERLAIMONT.	

Army Form C. 2118.

WAR DIARY

Headquarters,
38th Division, R.E.

INTELLIGENCE SUMMARY.

Sheet No.2.

(Erase heading not required.)

Instructions regarding War Diaries and Intelligence Summaries are contained in F. S. Regs., Part II. and the Staff Manual respectively. Title pages will be prepared in manuscript.

Place	Date	Hour	Summary of Events and Information	Remarks and references to Appendices
AULNOYE.	8th.		On 8th R.E.H.Qrs moved to AULNOYE, and R.E. and Pioneers were employed on road work and bridges over River SAMBRE. Work was done on road mine craters at C.4.d.8.6. and D.11.d.9.0. (both sheet 57.A.). Lt. Col. M.Whitwill, D.S.O., M.C., R.E. arrived for attachment to R.E.H.Qrs pending orders being received for him to take over the appointment of C.R.E., 38th (Welsh) Division vice Lt. Col. T.E.Kelsall, D.S.O., R.E. who is being sent to England for 6 months rest. From 10th the maintenance of the SAMBRE bridges was taken over by E.R.E., 33rd Division, 'e also taking over road maintenance as far east as the road inclusive which runs N.N.W. through U.30.a. and c. sheet 51. C.R.E., 38th Division took over road maintenance east of that. Pioneers and Field Companies were accordingly moved further east. In connection with filling in mine craters blown at culverts over running water (which was the commonest case), it was found that were trees were available, a good form of repair was as shown in sketch below. Logs. Tree Trunks. Water.	
AULNOYE.	15th.		Lt. Col. T.E.Kelsall, D.S.O., R.E. proceeded to England. Lt. Col. M.Whitwill, D.S.O., M.C., R.E assumed duties as C.R.E., 38th Division.	
	15th-22nd.		123 Field Coy R.E. employed on new Divn. Cinema at AULNOYE Station. 124 and 151 Field Coys R.E. continued work on road bridges at SOLRINNES, FLOURSIES, DIMECHAUX.	
	22nd.		All 38th Divisional Field Coys R.E. moved to BERLAIMONT.	
	26th.		Major General T.ASTLEY CUBITT, C.M.G., D.S.O., R.A., Commanding 38th (Welsh) Division inspected 38th Division, Royal Engineers and presented ribbons of decorations awarded to officers and other ranks.	

Leon Soya
Captain, & Adjt. R.E.
for C.R.E., 38th (Welsh) Division.

Army Form C. 2118.

WAR DIARY
or
INTELLIGENCE SUMMARY.

Headquarters,
38th Division R.E.

(Erase heading not required.)

Instructions regarding War Diaries and Intelligence Summaries are contained in F. S. Regs., Part II. and the Staff Manual respectively. Title pages will be prepared in manuscript.

Place	Date	Hour	Summary of Events and Information	Remarks and references to Appendices
VECQUEMONT.	Jany. 1919.		38th Divisional Engineers continued work on Hutted Camp for Infantry and R.A.Units. A large quantity of furniture was made at the C.R.E.Workshops, Chinese Labour and German prisoners were chiefly employed on this work. This work was considerably handicapped previously, due to not having a Circular Saw and Bench to cut up the Timber into smaller sizes. Two Circular Saw Benches were salved from the devastated area and also a large quantity of other valuable Machinery, and a portable Boiler & Engine. These were all erected at the C.R.E. Workshops. Instructional classes were started but only a small number of Students came forward for instruction, and the majority of these were not tradesmen; and special classes were arranged for the backward Students. Lectures were arranged but after a few weeks trial it was found they were not a success and Tradesmen and Apprentices now get individual instruction from the Adjutant R.E.each day. This method of teaching the men Engineering Subjects seems to be much more appreciated than the former method of Lectures as the men are more ready to ask for information and it enables the instructor to find out how much each man knows and what he wants to learn. During this month nearly all the experienced Tradesmen have been demobilized and it was very difficult to obtain good instructors to take charge of the various shops and classes. On the 30th January, Lieut-Col. M.WHITWILL, D.S.O., M.C., C.R.E., 38th Division was demobilized and proceeded to England. Major H.A.S.PRESSEY joined 27/1/19 to take over duties of C.R.E.	

Captain & Adjutant.R.E.
for C.R.E., 38th Division.

38th Division "G".
==================

        Herewith War Diaries from R.E.H.Q. and Field Companies, for February 1919.

3/3/19.

                                                Lieut-Col. R.E.
                                  C.R.E., 38th (Welsh) Division.

Army Form C. 2118.

WAR DIARY
or
INTELLIGENCE SUMMARY.
(Erase heading not required.)

Headquarters,
38th Division R.E.

Place	Date	Hour	Summary of Events and Information	Remarks and references to Appendices
VECQUEMONT.	1/2/19.		R.E.Headquarters at VECQUEMONT Chateau with Workshops at Vecquemont Railhead. R.E., Chinese, and German Labour employed at Workshops making furniture for Camps, also making large numbers of packing cases. Courses for Tradesmen continued but not very satisfactory due to Instructors and Students being demobilized. Field Companies continued work on Hutted Camps, but due to demobilization work considerably curtailed. H.R.H. The Prince of Wales visited R.E.Workshops on 7th inst. H.Q.R.E. demobilized to Cadre on 27/2/19.	

Lieut-Col,R.E.
C.R.E., 38th (Welsh) Division.

Army Form C. 2118.

WAR DIARY
or
INTELLIGENCE SUMMARY.

H.Q.R.E. 38th (Welsh) Division.

(Erase heading not required.)

Instructions regarding War Diaries and Intelligence Summaries are contained in F.S. Regs., Part II. and the Staff Manual respectively. Title pages will be prepared in manuscript.

Jul 39

Place	Date	Hour	Summary of Events and Information	Remarks and references to Appendices
VECQUEMONT.	1/3/19.		Strength H.Q. Officers 2. Other Ranks 5. Field Companies reduced to Cadre "A". Work on Hutting, in Workshops and at VECQUEMONT. Repairing damaged property where claims have been lodged by Civilians.	
	17/3/19.		Chinese Labour left R.E.Park.	
	5/5/19.		Captain W.A.EVANS, 151st Field Coy.R.E., left to join 200th Field Coy.R.E.	
	16/3/19.		Captain S.NORTH, 123rd Field Coy.R.E., left to join 219th Field Coy.R.E.	
	20/3/19.		2nd Lieut.M.C.RAY, 123rd Field Coy.R.E., left to join 458th Field Coy.R.E.	
	30/3/19.		Captain G.U.MORGAN, O.B.E., (Adjutant), reported to A.D.E.S.(West) DOULLENS for duty.	
	31/3/19.		Strength H.Q. Officers 1. Other Ranks. 5.	

Lieut-Col.R.E.,
C.R.E., 38th (Welsh) Division.

Army Form C. 2118.

WAR DIARY
or
INTELLIGENCE SUMMARY.
(Erase heading not required.)

H.Q.R.E. 38th (Welsh) Division.

Vol 40

Place	Date	Hour	Summary of Events and Information	Remarks and references to Appendices
VECQUEMONT.	1/4/19.		Strength H.Q. Officers 1. Other Ranks. 5.	
	6/4/19.		Major H.A.S.PRESSEY, M.C.R.E., 123rd Field Coy.R.E. proceeded to U.K.to report War Office, for instructions prior to proceeding to India.	
	6/4/19.		Lieut-Colonel I.W.MASSIE, M.C., R.E., granted Leave to U.K.from 7/4/19 to 21/4/19.	
	25/4/19.		Lieut.Colonel I.W.MASSIE, M.C., R.E., proceeded to take up appointment of C.R.E., CAUDRY Sub-Area.	
	30/4/19.		Strength H.Q. Officers Nil. Other Ranks. 4.	

[signature] Lieut.R.E.
for C.R.E., 38th Division.

Army Form C. 2118.

WAR DIARY
or
INTELLIGENCE SUMMARY.

H.Q.R.E., 38th (Welsh) Division.

(Erase heading not required.)

Instructions regarding War Diaries and Intelligence Summaries are contained in F. S. Regs., Part II. and the Staff Manual respectively. Title pages will be prepared in manuscript.

Place	Date	Hour	Summary of Events and Information	Remarks and references to Appendices
VECQUEMONT.	1/5/19.		Strength H.Q.R.E. 1 Officer. 5 Other Ranks. Packing and preparing Mobilization Stores for handing in to Ordnance on the Unit being disbanded.	
	31/5/19.		Lieut. A.G.DOYLE M.C., R.E. Commanding 123rd Field Company R.E. proceeded to U.K. for Repatriation to South Africa.	

Lieut. R.E.
for C.R.E., 38th Division.

Army Form C. 2118.

WAR DIARY
or
INTELLIGENCE SUMMARY.

(Erase heading not required.)

H.Q.,R.E.
38th (Welsh) Division.

Instructions regarding War Diaries and Intelligence Summaries are contained in F. S. Regs., Part II. and the Staff Manual respectively. Title pages will be prepared in manuscript.

Place	Date	Hour	Summary of Events and Information	Remarks and references to Appendices
VECQUEMONT.	4/6/19.		Handing in Unit Equipment to I.C.S.POULAINVILLE.	
	6/6/19.		Two releasable men proceeded to Vth Corps Demobilization Camp for Demobilization.	
	7/6/19.		Retainable personnel proceeded to C.R.E., 6th Division Rhine Army. Unit disbanded.	

Lieut.R.E.
for C.R.E., 38th (Welsh) Division.

www.ingramcontent.com/pod-product-compliance
Lightning Source LLC
Chambersburg PA
CBHW062359230426
43662CB00038B/2083